Dear Cousin

Governor's House at Sydney, Port Jackson, 1791, by William Bradley
Mitchell Library

Dear Cousin

The Reibey Letters

Twenty-two letters of Mary Reibey, her children and their descendants, 1792–1901

Edited and with commentary by

Nance Irvine

HALE
& IREMONGER

First published by Janet Press in 1992
© Nance Irvine 1992
This edition first published in 1995
10 9 8 7 6 5 4 3 2 1

COVER: Background photograph 'A direct North general View of Sydney Cove' by T. Watling held in the Dixson Galleries, State Library of New South Wales; Inset photo Miniature portrait of Mary Reibey, watercolour on ivory, 1777-1855, Mitchell Library, State Library of New South Wales. INSIDE COVERS: Mary Reibey letter; original held by the Mitchell Library, State Library of New South Wales and reproduced with their kind permission.

Printed and bound by
Southwood Press Pty Limited
80–92 Chapel Street, Marrickville, NSW

For the publisher
Hale & Iremonger Pty Limited
GPO Box 2552, Sydney, NSW

National Library of Australia Cataloguing-in-publication entry

Dear cousin: the Reibey letters: twenty two letters of the Reibey family 1792-1901: being a collection including letters of Mary Reibey, her children and their descendants.

Bibliography.
Includes index.
ISBN 0 86806 573 0 (pbk.)

1. Reibey, Mary, 1777-1855. 2. Reibey family — Correspondence.
3. Pioneers — New South Wales — Correspondence. 4. Pioneers — Tasmania — Correspondence. 5. New South Wales — History — 1788-1900 — Sources.
6. Tasmania — History — 1802-1900 — Sources. I. Irvine, Nance.
II. Reibey, Mary, 1777-1855.

994.40099

Contents

Acknowledgements to first edition

Without the contributions of 160 friends, including some 87 descendants of Mrs Mary Reibey, the State Library of NSW and its Book Shop, then I know, never would have flowed the apocryphal "blood, sweat and tears" required to complete this production of *Dear Cousin,* the Reibey Letters.

Therefore I am deeply grateful to all.

In particular, to Frances Atkinson of Hobart who encouraged with frequent moral support and money to cover the extra expenses, such as the pictures in the book; to historian and friend Paul Brunton, Curator of the Manuscripts, State Library of NSW, who has again given me his expert advice on such niceties that crop up when dealing with old family letters, as indeed have all his staff: to Rosemary Moon, Executive officer of our Library Society committee, who has given unstinting practical help: and to Vic Crittenden, historian and publisher, who from his wealth of experience, has patiently advised the newly fledged publisher, JANET PRESS. Without the original unselfish supply of copies of the Dear Cousin letters by the English descendants, Hibbert Binney of Sherborne, UK, and Oliver William-Powlett of Devon, there would never have been an attempt, by me, to make available a book of these letters; letters, now safely housed in the Manuscripts Department of the State Library of NSW.

Nance Irvine. Glebe. 1992.

Foreword

Mary Reibey's story *Dear Cousin* is a spectacular Australian "rags-to-riches" tale which even after 200 years still enthrals those who read it.

Mary Haydock. as she then was, arrived in Sydney as a convicted criminal in October 1792, having been sentenced to transportation for horse stealing at the age of 13.

She married a free settler, Thomas Reibey, in 1794, who on his untimely death in 1811 left his wife with seven children and his diverse business interests.

With such success did she pursue these interests that within five years she was reputed to be worth 20,000 pounds.

In 1820, she visited England with two of her daughters in some triumph — a respectable and wealthy woman — and kept a diary of this progress which can be read today in the Mitchell Library.

She died in 1855, just a few weeks after her 78th birthday, a legendary businesswoman who also took an active interest in community affairs.

In 1982, Nance Irvine published Mary Reibey's biography under the title "Mary Reibey: Molly Incognita." A revised edition was published in 1987 and remains in print.

Mrs. Irvine now presents us with "Dear Cousin," which reproduces the text of all Mary Reibey's extant letters.

Most of these are now held in the Mitchell Library, State Library of New South Wales. This is due in no small measure to Nance Irvine's inveterate pursuit of Australian historical manuscripts and her commitment to ensuring that they be placed in an appropriate repository where they will be accessible to all researchers.

A famous English contemporary of Mary Reibey, and one of that century's most lucid prose writers, John Henry Newman, asserted that "a man's life is to be found in his letters," and a woman's also. Reading Mary Reibey's letters gives us an insight into the life of a fascinating and heroic woman. We must hope that more of her letters will come to light perhaps as a result of this book.

Newman's motto as a cardinal was: "cor ad cor loquitur," heart speaks to heart. There is no better way to achieve this in the case of our forebears than in reading their letters.

Paul Brunton
Curator of Manuscripts
Mitchell Library, State Library of New South Wales. July 1992

for Vic Crittenden

1777– 1855
Miniature portrait of Mary Reibey
watercolour on ivory
Mitchell Library, State Library of New South Wales

Introduction

"It is to be the task of the historian... to tell the story of how the world came to be."
Manning Clark.

*I*t's time in this Bicentennial year of Mary Reibey's arrival that this collection should be available for all to read. Here are some 22 letters from Reibey family sources. They tell us a great deal about the Colony between 1792 and 1901. The young lass "just turned 15" arrived in Sydney Cove on the *Royal Admiral* in 1792, two hundred years ago. These letters are akin to light beacons during some of the formative years of New South Wales. Shelved carefully by their recipients the letters quietly bided the historian's slow search. Slow? Yes and tantalizing. But I was lucky. Like others of the Victorian era this family wrote prodigious communications to their kin. Hence the title *Dear Cousin.*

The Biography, *Mary Reibey: Molly Incognita* (published 1982-1987) brought to light a documented account of the events and of 1791, the year of the trial of Molly Haydock (later Mary Reibey); and of the subsequent happenings. Descendants began to seek me out. First letters to surface were two letters from Mary Reibey herself. Two lying discreetly amongst other missives within a small cardboard box belonging to Admiral Sir Peverill William-Powlett, a great great grandson of the lady. In that sitting room of the old manor house, Cadhay, I pointed out to the watching William-Powlett family, in 1982, the unmistakeable signature of Madam Mary Reibey, (previously copied by me from her signature in an old family bible held in Tasmania).

At that time there were no known letters of hers in Australia as I well knew. (So far all retrieved letters have been found in England.)

Proud of their enterprising convict forbear, this family most generously gave these two letters to the Mitchell Library manuscripts' department.

I had long suspected that Mary must have been corresponding with her own family connections so circulated the first edition of the Biography among known distant relatives. And so it came to pass as one might say, we have a collection.

An Australian reader spurred Mr Hibbert Binney of Sherbourne to search amongst his splendid collection of letters dating back to the 18th Century. Hibbert, now a close friend, is a great great grandson of Molly Haydock's Aunt Penelope Hope (Nee Law). His own mother and her mother had carefully (for nearly 200 years) stored her distant cousin's letters together with other memorabilia. Hibbert wisely took these letters to the expert Sotheby's for advice together with a copy of the biography. Magic indeed! Sotheby's sent me a copy of their sales advice together with a copy of probably the most important letter.. Molly's spirited note to her Aunt Hope. She wrote bravely from the transport *Royal Admiral* when finally anchored just inside Port Jackson.

In the event, the State Library of New South Wales bought some of the letters at the Sotheby Auction, adding to the now respectable collection. Negotiations still continue for this first letter.

The letters have been correlated with what information I have been able to extrapolate from contemporary sources.

Nance Irvine
Glebe, 1992

Father of Tom

*F*ascinating letters of Thomas Reibey's Father, Edward Raby/Reibey concerning the shipwreck of his boat the Tannah.

The interesting tale of Thomas Reibey (spelt Raby, Ribey and finally Reibey) husband of Mary/Molly Haydock.

Thomas was the first mate on the East India Co licensed whaler Britannia, captained by the part owner and friend of Tom, Captain Raven. By chance Mary and Tom's grandson, Thomas Reibey III, Premier of Tasmania, was interviewed by a (Hobart) Mercury in 1876 at Entally House, Hadspen, Tasmania. The newspaper account reveals how the house was named Entally, as was his parent's house in Macquarie Place Sydney, both after the district Entally near Calcutta in Bengal.

His grandfather, the Premier said, had been wrecked as a boy marine off the Bengal coast, rescued and cared for by the Bengal people at Entally.

He, Thomas, had believed his father was drowned. With this slim clue I searched in the India Office Library in Blackfriars Road, London, for evidence of wrecks off Bengal between the relevant years 1748 to 1800. Likewise I looked in the Press Lists of Calcutta from 1748 to 1800 and found the letters of Tom's father addressed to the East India Company after a spell as a prisoner of the French.. He was Edward Raby(for one spelling of Reibey) younger son of a Cobham Kent family, second officer of the East India Company schooner Tannah. This English vessel of the hated East India Company was caught by the French and burned to the water line on 24th January 1781. The boy, Thomas, escaped when wrecked. He was twelve years old and a midshipman on his father's boat. Fortunately, he was rescued by the Bengal family or people from Entally.

Tom, when Mary's spouse, remained a frequent visitor to Entally, Bengal, and eventually after his last visit in 1810, there contracted an illness which killed him in 1811. Edward Raby, Tom's father had been taken prisoner by the French, being released after the Treaty of Versailles of 1783. Edward Raby made his way to Fort William, the Calcutta Base of the East India Company only to find that all his friends were either dead or had returned to Europe. I quote the two letters as discovered in the India Office Library in London.

Fort William 23rd February 1794

Hon'ble Sir & Sirs,

I beg leave to lay before your Hon'ble Board that I was made prisoner by the French on 24th of January 1781, being at that time 2nd officer on board the TANNAH schooner, belonging to the Hon'ble Company's Bengal Marines and that after a severe imprisonment I am at length arrived at this place distitute of every necefsary where to add to mortifiucation those Friends I left here in whose power in was to assist me are either dead or gone to Europe. I therfore Hon'ble Sir Sirs look up to you for assistance hoping you will enable me by an order from your Hon'ble Board to receive my pay as second officer of the above mentioned Vessel during the time of my imprisonment to furnish myself with such necefsarys as I am immediately in want of/ trusting in the Generosity of the Hon'able Board.

I remain & ca Edward Raby

The order of the Hon'ble Board reads;

February 1784

Agreed that mr Raby be put on the same footing with others in a similar Situation and Ordered that notice thereof be sent to the Marine Paymaster.

Edward made his way home to England where he made his will naming his brother Alexander Raby, Gentleman of Cobham Kent as his executor. He returned on the Deptford 16th August 1786 to Diamond Head, port for Calcutta as a saloon passeger; he having first been to the top control in London of the Company's affairs to secure his promotion. Cudbert Thornhill, Supervisor of the Bengal marines wrote

" that on enquiry it appears that Mr Raby deserves to be reinstated with his rank as Officer commanding."

I can find no record of his death, certainly not on board the Deptford, no record of his marriage. But there can be little doubt that he was Tom's father after such evidence of Tom having been wrecked at that time as a Marine seaman. Interestingly Mary never sought out any Reibey connections when visiting England yet pursued every Haydock relative in 1820. Speculation as to coloured relatives was not encouraged. Even more interesting that Tom Reibey no.1 had such a strong affection for Entally, Calcutta. I tend to think that his mother was a high caste Indian lady as was the case with so many officers in the East India Company. He was always a brave sailor, suffering pirates, (Vide Sydney Gazette report) native uprising on the Pacific Islands as well as his experiences as a boy midshipman. Mary may never have know of Edward Raby, only of the Entally connection.

These newly found letters of the Reibeys and the Hopes, records of the East India Company and of the great Tom Reibey the III, Premier of Tasmania, solve the mystery.

Early Scenario to
The Tale of The Letters

*M*olly Haydock (later Mary Reibey of Sydney) the second daughter of the union of James Haydock with Jane Law, was born in 1777 in Bury, near Blackburn, Lancashire. Her family connections have names which are incredibly dynastic: Yeoman names as Hindle, Hope, Hargreaves, Law. They pop up repeatedly in the pale old parchment rolls covering some 400 years of christenings, marriages and deaths prepared long ago by the good Bishop of the Parish of Walter le Dal. Bury, contiguous to Darwen, a Norman settlement in the 11th century, became the village and home of some 600 coal cutters in 1702. But by Moly's time Bury was a thriving 18th century town of some 3587 souls, according to available records. Nearby Manchester boasted a population of 140,000, albeit connected with other centres by a muddy track flattened by unwieldly carts. On the main route from Liverpool, itself a hive of shipping industry, this Blackburn district was well aware of highwaymen seeking a fortune from venturesome coach travellers. Gibbets were standing in public places, often with a swinging tenant; some unlucky villain caught practising grand and/or petty larceny.

Smuggling was a career job; a small packet of tea was a welcome gift, no questions asked by respectable folk. The Haydock families and kin, sound Yeoman stock, lived out their uncomplicated lives in this busy area. Unremarkable that is until niece Molly was stranded, alone! Orphaned as a babe she had been fortunately cared for by her Mother's family. Indeed she had been well schooled at the Blackburn Grammar School and instructed in all desirable church habits by her grandma Law... deceased in 1790. Now rejected by her family, enrolled in some heartily disliked institution Molly fled the coop. Molly explored the vagaries of the highway. She became a skiful vagabond. Bright enough indeed to roam for months, successfully disguised as a boy, under the pseudonym of James Borrow, a recently deceased playmate.

Caught some months later in Stafford while attempting to "flog" a horse stolen from distant Chester "the boy" had to endure life in a contemporary mixed prison of Stafford, followed by a trial in August 1791.

Tried for the heinous crime of horse stealing, punishable by the Death sentence, and thereby breaking the peace of King George III the Judge sentenced the vagabond prisoner, presumed to be a boy, to death by hanging. This condemning was transmuted to seven years across the seas to Botany Bay as " the boy was so small, so young." Upon the final hosing down before embarking, Molly's charade as a "boy" was rumbled, blown!

Hastily the Haydock family came to the party and a white washing Petition for the girl's release was sent to the King's advisers. The Trial judge rejected the petition as no member of the Blackburn family would undertake to care for the girl for the ensuing 4 years. Moreover His honor thought there had been a fair trial and the young person was pretty cunning! As we know the young person made a fairly healthy journey from Plymouth to Sydney Cove, arriving on the Royal Admiral on 7th October in1792. Married in 1794 to First Mate Thomas Reibey of Britannia of the East India Co. After a successful 17 years together, sadly she became a widow with 7 children. Mary Reibey lived to become Sydney's first woman entrepreneur, large land owner, builder of much of original lower George Street, farming through her sons much of the NSW south coast and Northern Tasmania.

Emancipist woman though she was, Mary Reibey bravely supported the creation of our first bank, the Bank of New South Wales (now Westpac), providing her dwelling in Macquarie Place as the base office. She deserves an acknowledged and distinguished place in our early history records, a great pioneer of early Australia.

West view of Sydney-Cove taken from the Rocks, at the rear of the General Hospital
Dixson Galleries

North-west view taken from the Rocks above Sydney, in New South Wales, for
John White, Esqr., by Thomas Watling

Letter 1

*F*rom the young convict, Mary Haydock to her Aunt Hope.

This first letter, for me, has all the charm of a young girl, a little apprehensive but determined to survive in this odd distant land.

Much valuable information is packed into the letter written 8th October 1792 on her last day on board Royal Admiral. It may very well be one of several written by her and "posted" from Rio, from Cape Town[1]. This assumption is valid as she does not, here, mention her companions nor describe any event of the long sea voyage almost as if she has written all about it earlier. Apart from reports from Collins and Phillip, some details of the voyage are known from contemporary and existing letters by two men, passengers on board. The letters were sent from these Atlantic ports. One from James Lacey[2] a literate convict and one from Gunner George Thompson[3].

Mary and the other women were relatively well cared for. Thompson's other job was to assist Surgeon Alley in the care of the 289 convict men and 48 women. All squeezed on board this tiny ferry-sized sailing boat, along with spare masts, shipping gear, stores including caged live food, and of course the crew... He also supervised the fair distribution of ship's rations.

Gunner Thompson was revered by the convicts. He wrote of and named six very young convicts in his care, three boys and three girls including the youngest small girl, adding this Latin tag:

'Quis talio fando temperete lachrymis'

Finally there is 'Scott' only 13 years 'who saying such things could refrain from tears' (Virgil)

Presuming that her North Lancashire accent was mistaken for a scottish burr the account points squarely to Mary Haydock recorded as "119 Mary Haddock" in the ship's muster. Again allow for the accent of the Lancashire lass. Moreover she was the youngest teenager on board. In her portraits as a mature woman she is shown as small and short necked., James Lacey wrote from the Cape 19th August 1792 in a long account of the voyage from England to the Cape.. (to an unidentified friend in high place, who was caring for the Lacey's child in England);

of Mr Thompson... the greatest praise falls short of what this gent'ln deserves for his unremitted attention to the health and comfort of the unhappy men under his care...

Lacey also complains that his wife, has had to mix with the women convicts. She was a free woman who has made the long voyage to be near her convicted husband. He writes;

> None of the women (convicts) are deceaased, which may be in a great measure imputed to their being under no restraint or confinement, their situation being not only superior to men convicts, but likewise to those denominated (free) passengers, women accompanying their husbands...

Three days after the arrival of Royal Admiral, *Govenor Phillip reported to Secretary Dundas:*

> Of the convicts embarked on that ship, ten men and two women died on the passage and four children were born, one of whom died.. seventy two men, eleven women and five children have been landed sick. I have no doubt but that..strict justice has been done to (the passengers) but.. I think the people have been too much crowded on this ship [4]

Mary ipso facto, has to have witnessed much close loving and quarrelling in such a small tight world; to have assisted at birthing, dying amongst the people.

And still more detail from a contemporary. David Collins, Judge Advocate and Secretary of the Colony who kept a journal from the day he sailed with the first fleet, and has left valuable comments about the colonial happenings. So we know that on 7th October,

> Royal Admiral, East Indiaman commanded by Captain Essex Henry Bond anchored in the cove from England whence she sailed on the 30th May last. Her passage from the Cape of Good Hope was the most rapid ever madde, being only five weeks and three days from port to port. On board.. came stores and provisions.. one sergeant, one corporal and nineteen privates belonging to the New South Wales Corps; a person to be employed in the cultivation of the country, another as a master miller, and a third as a master carpenter... She brought in with her a fever which

had been much abated by the extreme attention paid by Captain and his officers to cleanliness.. the sick.. eighty, were all immediately dissembarked from the Indiaman; the remainder of her convicts were sent up to be employed at Parramatta...

So much for the background of the voyage which is essential to our understanding of the first letter. That Captain Bond set up temporary private shops at Parramatta, Toongabbie and Sydney Cove selling forbidden spirits under the name of porter, and selling many goods to a goodly profit to the tune of 3600 Seventeenth century English pounds is not really relevant to these records, but very interesting. That the arrival of the ship's stores did alleviate some of the harsh rationing maybe is important.
The lass Mary Haydock, the writer, is obviously well and is surveying the beautiful harbour on a spring day, on the second day of their arrival at a harbour which she and all arriving convicts mistakenly called "bottany bay"
Listen to what Acting Judge Richard Atkins in Sydney town reported on that day;

Hot weather, Wind East, about 12 heard distinctly 15 guns,.. hourly expect an account of a ship's arrival.

According to this letter the women had been told what to expect, more or less. Their chores would include making 4 pairs of trowsers per week. Their ration included one pound of rice per week and 4 pounds of pork. We know that it was salt pork mostly 2 to 3 years old.
Mary doesn't mention the parlous plight of these women arriving to fill a difficult vacuum.. about 6 men to one woman according to the records. Perhaps she had not realised. However George Thompson is quite definite;

the women have a more comfortable life than the men. Those who are not fortunate enough to be selected for'wives' which every officer, settler and soldier is entitled to, and few are without, are made hut keepers; those who are not dignified with this office are set to make shirts, frocks, trowsers, etc for the men at a certain number perday; occasionally to pick grass in the fields, and for a very slight offence are kept constantly at work the same as the men.

and from another anonymous and contemporary writer

the female convicts on their arrival are treated in the same manner as the males.. being well washed and furnished with a change of suitable apparel. The commissioned Officers come on board.. stand on deck, select such females as are most agreeable in their person who generally upon such occasions endeavour to set themselves off to the best advantage

In any case Mary writes:

so I must Conclude we are in a hurry to go ashore

Now Thomas Reibey, First mate on Britannia, a store ship, was in Sydney Cove assisting to prepare the vessel for Major Grose' chartered journey to Cape Town for food supplies. Did Tom have time to meet Mary? Was she sent with the healthy convicts to Parramatta? Was she indeed made a hut keeper ? No-one really knows. In September 1794, two years later she and Thomas married, she still under sentence for another four years. Did she happen to be made a housekeeper for Lieutenant Govenor Grose, he about to take over from the sick Phillip ? Later, in 1820 she made her way to England and visited the second Mrs Grose, both women of Sydney Cove, both widowed. In a later letter she infers that she met Thomas when she arrived in Sydney. Maybe. She is recorded as a housekeeper. That she did not serve an officer or settler as a 'wife' is pretty obvious as there is no child born to her according to the records. Later she bore 7 children to her husband Thomas Reibey.

The most interesting detail of this first letter is possibly the conning of her by a Mr Scott, extracting two of her precious guineas. I guess that was the last time that Mary Haydock..Reibey was ever cheated of money. Her affectionate farewell to her family makes me believe that there are still more letters of this first period awaiting discovery.

No liberties have been taken at all with the textual spelling or punctuation. With the exception of the occasional placing of a / to indicate the normal new sentence. Mary in common with many 18th century people omitted full stops.

As supplied by the original owner Mr. Hibbert Binney. 1987

The First Letter. From Mary Haydock to her Aunt Hope, Church Street, Blackburn, Lancashire.

octb 8th 1792

my Dear aunt

we arrived he on the 7th and I hope it will answer better than we expected for I write this on Board of ship but it looks a pleasant place-Enough / we shall but have 4 pair of trouser to make a week and we shall have a pound of rice a week and 4 pound of pork besides Greens and other vegetaibles / the tell me I am for life wich the The Governor told me I was but for 7 years wich Grives me very much to think of it but I will watch every oppertunity to get away in too or 3 years/ But I will make myself as happy as I can In my present and unhappy situation / I will Give you Further satisfaction when I Get there and is settled / I am well and hearty as ever I was in my life / I Desire you will answer me by some ship that is Coming and lett ma know how the Children is and all inquireing frinds / so I must Conclude because we are in a hurry to go a shore / remember My Love to my sister and aunt wamsley and My cousinbs so no more at pressent from your undutifull neice Mary Haydock / Mr Scot Took 2 Ginnues of me and said he would get me My Libberty / with my sister has been very ungood To me so I must never see you again /

NOTES

1. Rio and Cape Town were regular ports of call to replace supplies, wood for cooking, and water
2. James Lacey HRNSW Vol 2, 479
3. Thompson, George: An Account of the Miseries at Botany Bay 1794
4. Govenor Phillip to Dundas. HRNSW vol1, part 2, p665 11/10 1792 Atkins, Richard, Journal 1792-1810

Letter 2

Sydney NSW August 12, 1818.

Mary's Report..26 years further Down The Track. 1818
As yet 1991, I have not found records from these missing years.

Yet here we have a friendly family letter to England, to Alice her cousin and contemporary of Mary Reibey. Written as though well known to her cousin. But of course written some 26 years after the young convict girl's arrival in Sydney Cove, it reveals a hectic business life of the 1800s...

1792-1818

What happened ?

With a sketchy picture from reliable sources some of the 26 years' interregnum can be filled in. On 1st September 1794, by the Rev Richard Johnson Mary Haydock was married to First Mate, Thomas Reibey, ex Britannia, with his Captain's permission. Granted a small holding of 50 acres as a married man, (listed Land grant no 310) they settled in November 1794 on the banks of the Hawkesbury River. One can happily extrapolate the delight of the little 17 year old convict bride-girl and the seagoing Thomas with their fresh start in life. In contemporary drawings the usual quarters appear to have been a cottage of two rooms. Mostly made of clay plastered on pliant wattle branches with an earth floor the tiny kitchen would have had a skillion kitchen, separated from the rooms for reasons of fire safety.

The Reibeys survived Aboriginal attacks and heavy floods. Two sons were born on the Hawkesbury, Thomas Haydock Reibey and James Haydock Reibey. By marketing, trading and the shrewd mortaging of failed settlers, the Reibeys prospered and finally moved on to Sydney. Thomas became a shipbuilder with his partner Wills.

He captained his own ship, trading with the 'Feejees,' so called. Mary ran a successful store. Seven children were born, the last a girl named Elizabeth arrived only months before the early death of Thomas in April 1811, aged 42 years. The family were living in their Grand New House, Entally, lot 70 in Macquarie Place Sydney.

Undaunted the widowed Mrs Reibey aggressively continued to manage her late husband's business. More vessels were built; grants of land and purchases of property were all part of her trading empire. She helped to set up the bank of NSW, allowing the use of her house as an initial headquarters. She sent her two eldest boys 'home' to England for some education. The Bond store, which accomodated some of her imports, still(1992) stands in the Rocks area.

Now to her letter.

She had sponsored her sister Eliza with her family and husband Charles Foster. This family was granted land nearby to Launceston, Van Diemens Land. Mary's eldest boy, Thomas Reibey II had settled on a wondrous grant in the Esk River, at Hadspen and site of the historic Entally mansion. He had taken for a bride the lovliest English girl in Sydney, Richarda Allen and in "a fairy tale come true" sort of way, brought *her to Van Diemens Land in his own ship, built in his family's ship yards. Mary travels to VDL in her own brig commanded "by my son Thomas".*

   Her emancipated status appears to be well buried in her business facade.

   And yet the lady bemoans the curiousity of gossips.

   Lachlan Macquarie was a favourite. He showed a balanced approach to the emancipist question; one wonders if he was privy to the wealthy widow's status.

   Mary is planning in 1818 to sail to her old mother land; to bring her daughter Celia, perhaps the young girls and possibly George. As you can read, the question is with what English tutor shall she place son George? What sweet revenge on society! George has had some Latin instruction.

   Note the evidence of the keen merchant she was. There is a lament for the falling off of trade. Her letter lists her properties and income in this year 1818.

   Her statement of her original meeting with her husband is ambiguous but totally adaptable. After all they did meet in Sydney before September, 1794.

   Mary did travel to England in 1820 with Celia and Eliza.

   Mary Reibey at this stage had acquired property in NSW, both at the Hawkesbury and on the South Coast, in Sydney, Lower George Street, Hunters Hill, later at Newtown and in Tasmania.. apart from two cottages in Lancashire (UK)

   Her cousin David Hope attended to her affairs such as merchandising enterprises in the UK.

From Mary Reibey in Sydney to her Cousin Alice Hope, Lancashire

Sydney, NSW August 12, 1818

Dear Cousin,

by a Gentleman Who Expects to come to Liverpool and which I believe is a resident thier I avail myself of the opportunity of letting you know that with myself my Family are all well and that of Announcing the safe arrival of my dear sister and Family all well except herself which suffered severely during a passage of Five months and 2 days / but now thank God she is perfectly Recovered / and which more added to her dissapointment was when she arrivd I was absent at Vandiemans Land whither I had gone to settle my affairs previous to my Coming home as I had Let my shop and Whare houses as also my Farms / but her arrival will detain me sometime longer as I do not wish to leave her / and Mr Foster Expects to get his Land and Indulgences and proceed with the cultivation of it so that he can either let it or sell it / I intend bringing my Eldest Daughter Celia and youngest son George and I believe my three little ones... that I am present Deveided about my son George I was thinking of placing with Mr... of Manchester / Should we Agree & should it lye in your way to mention it to him I Whould thank you to send his Terms so that I may hasten his Comeing home as he is getting so big / I had him at a Latin School till within this 9 months / ever since he *(Tom?)* came from England my eldest Son is married *(to Richarda Allen)* became the father of a fine daughter *(Mary Allan Reibey later married to Charles Arthur)* / my other Son James which I let your ever Revered Mother know of his Marriage *(Internal evidence of communications with the Hopes prior to this letter)* is now on a visit to us and on business / but George is now at Vandiemans Land as I left him to Collect the Remainder of my Debt and rents / when I heard my sister had arrived I was very Impatient to see her so that she has not yet seen him / I went down their *(Van Diemen's Land)* in a brig of my own commanded by my Son Thomas and brought her up *(to Sydney)* Loaded with which she is now gone *(to Newcastle ?)* after a cargo of Cedar Wood for Building / Mr Foster is gone in her I expect him in the Course of six or Eight weeks / I have also got a Small Schooner but Trade and Commerce is getting so bad that I cannot sell anything or I should have been Home *(UK)* long before now / I have enclosed you a Couple of our Sydney Gazettes where you will see an advertisement of mine but their is no person here able to purchase them / so I must give over the Idea of selling and live on my income / but I had forgot 2 Farms one of 100 & one of 40 acres at the Hawkesbury and the Estate that I have lately purchased at Vandiemans Land of 2000 as an entail on my children forever and one Agoing I purchased when i was down their of 40 acres / so that my yearly income is one Thousand pounds and should I Come to England immediately I could have Remitted Home *(UK)* seven hundred pounds per Annem after leaving a little for my sons and paying agency - therefore I think it will be as well to leave them as to Sell as to make a sacrifice / my sister begs me to mention a Book Entitle the History of N.S Wales that she left with a man Byron's next door to the first House as you turn the Corner / that is all the description she can give / she wishes you to get it for her if you Can / she would do very well here Could she have her own way at her Business and Mr Foster too but no one will do well that is not thrifty Correct and Sober / this place is not like England / you are under the Eye of every one and your Character Scrutinized by both Rich and poor altho you may have a different Oppinion of it through the Different Characters that Comes here but are kept in regular order by our Good Govenor Lachlan Macquerie / he has been here these eight years altho it is the orders from home that no Govt should be kept here more than five years but through his good Conduct is Solicited from England to Stay Longer / the young man that I wrote my sister sometime ago by the Name of James Foster Which she tells me she understood to be the same person which Mrs Hilton Interceded for is doing very well and a very Respectable young man he is / before my sister Came he told me he knew your Brother John very well / those Houses in Salford which did belong to me & my sister and which she has made over her Interest in to your Mother I should wish if agreeable to Repurchase on my arrival in England / the Bill is against me I have Rec'd by the hands of my sister which shall be attended too / I can assure you my poor sister never mentions your Mother but with Tears and the Deepest Sorrow for her loss and altho I had not seen her for 27 years it had a great effect on me for almost the first interchange of words with my sister was to know if my Aunt Hope was alive / I do assure you the meeting of her was one of the happiest moments of my life and still more so knowing it was in my power to assist her as I consider her so deserving the protection of me and everybody who knows her / She did not meet as good Treatment as might be expected on her passage Considering what she paid / but had I been at home while the Capt of the ship was here I whould have actioned him but he sailed the day after I came home... / little Eliza and James *(Aunt Foster's children)* go to the same school as my 3 children who are Boarders / they are fine company for each other/ little Eliza is... notice by everyone she is such an agreeable little thing / my youngest little girl *(Elizabeth)* and her are much alike and is remarked almost by everyone / my sister wished me particularly to mention to you how my Husband came here / he was 2d officer and ... of the Britannia Whaler which was laying in the Harbour when I came here and he prevailed on the Captain to let him stay here. *(Thomas Reibey served on the Britannia for two more voyages before leaving the ship... see Mary Reibey... Molly Incognita).*

I hope dear Cousin altho unknown to you but for the sake of your dear Mother you will write by every opportunity and by sending your letters to Mrs Smith in London where my sister stayd She will be remitted. / I have nothing more at present to say except my sons and all my children desire their love to you and all your brothers / my sister desires her Respectful Compliments to Miss Ward, Mrs Wood, Mrs Aspinall, Mrs Parkinson and my Aunts Hind and Ramsbottam and to all Inquiring Friends and pray Remember me to them likewise and my sincere love to yourself and brothers Jane and Eliza send their love to you

I am Dear Cousin yours affectionately

M.Reibey

My sister thinks it whould be the best way to pay the postage to the Lands end of England and they are sure to come safe..

This letter was recognised by me in 1981 in a collection at Cadhay, home of Sir Peveril William-Powlett great great grandson of Mary Reibey.

Oliver William-Powlett and his family generously gave these letters to the Manuscripts Department of the Mitchell Library.

Sketch of Mrs. Reibey's Farms in NSW - 1820

Credited to Cousin David Hope's office, Blackburn.

Nº of Farms	Situated	Names Tenants	Leases. to run	Nº of Acres	Present Rental	Expected. New Rental
1	On the banks of the Hawkesbury	T.McKenna	1 year	200	£85	£120
1	"	I.Dodds	5	40	20	30
	"	"	4	30	35	55
*1	"	T.Hampstead	4	30	50	65
*1	"	I.Armstrong	4	30	50	65
*3	"	A.Earley	3	80	65	90
1	"	An Irish man	3	100	35	50
1	"	Not let waste		100	nothing	80
1	on the district	J.Chippendale	7	200	of Airds	
20	Van Diemens Land	Sundries	var	2040	360	655

only about 600 acres cultivated yet

HOUSES IN SYDNEY

Warehouses & Stores George Street		Sundries	355	380		
House occupied by the Bank			3	150	160	
				*Acres=2920	1205	1800

*Excellent Farms.

The Diary

Commentary on a Traveller's Intermittent Notes, 1820-1821

One of the Foster descendants presented the Mitchell archives with this tiny note book. It is haphazardly written; a mixture of domestic reminders as "books for George", 2/6 owing to shop, and some irregular comments on the meetings with her Haydock and Law extended families. Together with lots of lovely descriptions, as Mary saw things, of London, Glasgow and Edinburgh.

For in 1820, as a wealthy widow from the antipodes, Mary finally returned to conquer her old stamping ground in the north west of England. With the two eldest girls, Celia and Eliza, she made the long voyage. Son Thomas and Richarda at Entally in VDL were responsible for the little girls, Jane Penelope and Elizabeth. George was working on his property. James also lived nearby in VDL: he, despite his mother's opposition, was most happily married to a young widow, Rebecca Breedon.

As we can see by reading the account of her properties, rents et al, Mary had left her affairs in good order, despite the recession of 1811-1812. She was indeed a wealthy widow.

Fascinating facets of her daily experiences, both in the U.K. and back in Sydney, surface when reading these simple entries. Demonstrably Mary had probably never visited nor enjoyed London during her early years, 1777-1790, in Blackburn and Bury, prior to transportation. Yet in 1820 with all the poise achieved and used in managing her multi-business affairs in New Sourth Wales she tackles the legendary capital city, its business houses and many streets. Moreover it is interesting to note how sea captains at anchor on the Thames, celebrated her visit.

So excited at returning to her own land, worried by the great metropolis! Never lacking in spirit she took a hackney coach to the required address to handle her business. She was a merchant of considerable power in Sydney. The Sydney business personnel of the early 1800's despite long delays in correspondence, were probably much closer to their head business offices in England, then were many Australians of the early twentieth century.

Accordingly trading firms and sea captains would welcome Mary's visit. In this first memo she meets old friends and the father of daughter Jane Penelope's first and only love, John Atkinson of New South Wales.

All three women were quite ill after the long voyage, requiring medical treatment such as, the 18th century "bleeding". That doesn't stop the all absorbing excitement of the new experiences. The visit noted on July 17, to the two theatres (including Covent Garden) viewing the obligatory three "pieces" of the time, is evidence of Mary's determination to "do" London.

And so to Lancashire.

A matter of interest for me was the long milage they often travelled in coaches without resting other than to change horses, for example London to Manchester: and later in Scotland.

I wonder at the tremendous welcome given by all the cousins; of course well warranted. But where were all the extended family when Molly Haydock so despereately needed help way back in 1791? At Blackburn the great support came from Cousin Alice ,daughter of the Draper Adam Hope who in 1791, had headed the unsuccessful Petition to have the girl's sentence reversed.

The visit in Preston to Horrocks Mill, presumably one of the original cotton weaving mills of the Industrial Revolution, was all part of Mary's intense interest in merchandise. She followed that up with a visit in Liverpool to the mechanical ironing of the muslin in a Liverpool factory.

According to these jottings in her note book the Social customs in the genteel houses of Edinburgh and Glasgow were practised by her various hostesses, the most endearing being the little dances, "balls", given in the comfortable living rooms. Not to mention the card games for the chaperones.

We are suitably reminded of the advances of scientific studies; she marvels at the camera obscura of Glasgow, the magnifing glass magnified 1400 times. Her desire to put her daughters in the hands of a contemporary finishing school in Edinburgh is of course de rigueur for candidates in the early nineteenth century marriage market. Mary Reibey understood all the intricacies of upward mobility.

Their portraits I think refer to the miniatures now held in the Mitchell Library. Especially as later in these notes Mary mentions that she has received her miniature frames.

But she had become an Australian in her political viewpoint…rather than merely a settler. Knowing of the endeavour to get self government in a limited way, we can well imagine why she spent so much time talking to WC Westworth, then visiting London. Three years later her son's letters are full of the political situation of the 1820s.

She details the difficulty of organizing her return trip to New South Wales; the final waiting at Gravesend for the Mariner, to collect them all. Both Eliza and Celia opt to return to N. S.Wales; the finishing school at Edinburgh offers too many cold baths, early rising as well as lessons in Art.

Lieut Thomson, distant relative of a famous Glasgow preacher, attached himself to the threesome. He, in fact accompanies them to Sydney, intent on marrying Eliza. Later he became an embezzler, as outlined in his brother-in-law's letters. However Mary's daughter, Eliza, stood by her husband and large family. There are many worthy descendants who have made the Thomson family a revered and long established Australian clan. The Reibeys akin to many early 19th century settler families, have generated for Australia, a solid tradition.

The ship Harriet in Tor Bay, 1819, by Thomas Whitcombe

1803 – 1823
Mrs. Celia Wills née Reibey
Watercolour on ivory
Mitchell Library, State Library of New South Wales

Mary's last entry is made on Thursday 5th July, 1821.

Mary Reibey 'fudged' her 1828 Census return, impying that she came free, had arrived in the Colony in 1821 by the Mariner. And we know she arrived in the Colony on 7th October 1792. Well, she lived at a time when emancipist was a dirty word, when a woman and a widow had to work hard at her image as an upright, God-fearing woman. This she did. Her Traveller's Notes are well worth savouring.

NOTES

Mr Jones was her London agent.
Mary was in pursuit of recompense for her daughter-in-law (Rebecca Reibey, wife of James) for the loss of her husband, - Breedon, of the military.

The Diary as Recorded by Mary Reibey 1820-1821

1820. June 20th Landed at Portsmouth 8 o'clock in the morning. Took refreshment at the Inn. Set of at 9 o'clock in the coach for London.

Arrived ther at 7 in the afternoon, at the Belle Savage Inn, Ludgate Hill. Took lodgings their. Wrote to Capt Watson, my friend to procure me lodgings but through an omission in my letter of my address, he could not find me out, therefore was obliged to stay their for 3 nights, not liking to go to a strange place. Next morning after I arrived I took hackney coach and went to the office of Bell & Wilkinson having business there. After my arrival the first person I saw to my great astonishment was Mr. Jones who was as much amazed as I was to see me in London. However sat down and had a little talk about our Country and in came Mr. Underwood and of course another wonder was pronounced how I came their. I had then delivered my papers to Mr. Jones who was kind enough to say he would do anything he could and I thought it would be better had he understood the Treasury better than I where I was going after...if I had not found him their. Mr. Underwood walked back with me to my lodgings and took me and my daughters out a little to see the Town. Treated us to Ice-cream and returned with us again, and left us immediately. I was then very anxious about Capt.Watson not comeing not knowing that I had forgot to give him my address. However it so happened that I had a letter from Mr. Atkinson to his father which I mentioned to some person who told him and the old Gentleman came immediately and a finer one and a better man their cannot be. He was very much affected when he read the letter and I believe it was very Favourable to me and Daughters as he immediately asked us to his House and have kept on friendship ever since. He mentioned to Capt. Watson where we was and on the Sunday morning being the third day after our arrival at the Inn he and his Two Daughters and Capt. Watson came to take us away as he has got lodgings for me next door to himself. During the time they was comeing to meet me (I had taken Coach and drove off for his House when Mrs.Watson kindly asked us in, dinner was prepared for us. In about a half an hour in came Capt. Watson and very glad he was to see us. After we had dined he called a Coach and we went to the Inn, settled my account and took my baggage to my Lodging it being pretty generally known by our Sydney friends and those who had visited Sydney as Capt. of ships and otherwise of our arrival in London and we had a great deal of visitors. I then wrote to my cousin John Hope in Manchester prior to our going down to the Country, but did not receive an answer in Course, owing to his having been removed about a mile and a half out of town, but hearing their was a letter for him in the Post office he immediately answered it by a very kind and affectionate letter and an invitation to stay at his house.

July 17 During our stay in London we visited the two Theatres where we saw the Provoked Husband after... Covent Gardens, the Obitiquary. after piece the Millar and his men. We did not visit many of the Public buildings owing to our being so ill. We had a medical Gentleman, Dr. White attending us upward of a fortnight who paid great attention to us. we arrived on the 20th June and left the 17th of July for the country making our stay their 27 days and the day before our departure for the country I was bled and blistered and both me and Eliza so ill...Celia was not much better

July 18 to August 6th. We arrived in Manchester the day following after l86 miles without stopping except to change horses. When we came to the Mosely Arms we found my two cousins Mr. Hargreaves, Surgeon and Druggist and Mr. John Hope waiting with a hackney coach to take us and Baggage to our Cousin Hope's a very delightful place a little way in the Country, where a Surgeon was sent for, Dr. Barton, a friend of my cousin Hargreaves, who took a great interest in recovering us as soon as possible. he paid all attention was possible, we began to recover fast and Mr. Hargreaves very oflten came to take us out walking. He sent us jellys, preserves and fruit and everything he could think of for comfort. As soon as we could walk about which was about ll days we had several invitations, the first to Dr. Barton's, one of the first Surgeons in Manchester. Mrs B. a very ladylike woman and one of the most respectable about that Country was very glad to see us and treated us very kindly wishing us to renew our visit as often as we could. We took tea with my half cousin, Mr. Aspinall. Dined and tead next day with Mr. and Mrs. Hargreaves, they made me promise on my return to Manchester that we should stop at their House. We staid at Manchester from the 8th of July to the 6th of August, being 19 days.

August 6th, We took the coach for Blackburn on the 6th where we arrived about 3 o'clock in the afternoon. Mr. john Hope accompany us. It is impossible to describe the sensations I felt when comeing to the top of Derwen Street my native home and amongst my relatives and on entering my once Grandmother's House where I had been brought up and to find it nearly the same as when I left nearly 29 years ago, all the same furniture and most of them standing in the same place as when I left but not one person I knew or knew me...but was fully requited by my Cousin Miss Hope who...met us at the door with all the affection and love of a sister.

Their being beds prepared for us we became a part of the family as we had already done at her brother's in Manchester. My arrival became known to all the old inhabitants of Blackburn who had known me in my Childhood, the door hardly ever closed with people comeing out of curiosity or respect...I had often expressed a wish to see my Children confirmed in the old Church at Blackburn. We arrived there on the Saturday evening and the Bishop on the Monday following (who only comes every three years). My cousin John Hope procured certificates from the Curate of St. John's and they was admitted and was confirmed with about 300 more males and females in St. John's Church, the old church being shut up.

August 8th. During the time we were at Blackburn we was divided betwixt my father's and Mother's relations. We had a general invitation in all their houses, especially Mr. William Haydock, son of my Uncle William who is in his 74th year and Mr. Robert Brown, son of my Aunt Hindle Brown who is in her 76th year. I believe they thought they could not show me enough of attention but no place was so congenial to my mind as Miss Hope's, the most affectionate young woman I ever met with...we met Mr. and Mrs. Little an independent Gentlemen who is one of the trustees to my Aunt Hope's estate...John Hope and he to settle our little business relation to the Houses...Mr. David Hope came...to Blackburn accord to his promise (27th August)...Was very proud to see each other and I found him to be one of the most affectionate. men I ever met with, quite a man of business too.

Sept. 5th. Took tea at Mr. Wraith's next day and whent to see the first stone laid of the old church at Blackburn. It is somewhat singular that nearly 30 years ago before that Mr. David Hope and myself was at the Sept laying of the first stone in St. John's Church.

Sept. 7th left for Preston...arrived at Preston in an hour and half...in a post chaise.

15th Sept. ...went to see Mr. Horrocks Mill and one of the proprietors showed us all through it, a most grand sight but the heat from the steam engine being too oppressive for me gave me a complete surfeit...to Blackburn...where I was taken very ill...at my Cousin's,Mr. Robert Brown...My Aunt Hindle Brown an old women in her 76th year would insist on sitting up with me part of the night...to see concern and attention was admd...

From Liverpool went to Greenock Glasgow by the Robert Bruce, Steam boat Left Liverpool Tuesday, arriving one o'clock Friday.

October 21,22,23...Rained very hard...wet feet...a violent cold.

Oct.24 Whent to the Museum, passed through the Cottage to the High Church, a very grand Cathedral built by the Roman Catholics 700 years ago., a very interesting sight it was. Whent to tea at Mr. Fleming, Mr. Hope's partner. Had a little dance among the young people.

Oct 25th Wednesday whent to the see the manufactorys of making cotton balls spinning machines. We took a walk around the Clyde ...passed the Roman Catholic Chaple, a very grand building .. the Gaol a very spaciuous building. Ill for 11 days .. the doctor's bill being Five Pounds three shillings and sixpence .. very exhorbitant demand I was bled with leeches at my temple ..

November 14th went to see a singeing iron that the muslin runs over and touching never damages the cloth altho red hot .. saw company at Mr Hopes an illumination and bonfire took place on account of the bill being thrown out against the Queen ..

15 November Celia sat for her picture, Captain Wood called and took us to see the Lunatic Asylum took a walk in Trongate and Argyle Street to see the spendid illumination.

Nov 15 this day I sat for my picture, my two daughters went trades hall .. a lecture on Education of Roman Catholic childen which the Protestant clergy has undertook providing they will allow the Bible to be read.

Nov 17 Went this day to Paisley, Manufacturing town about 6 miles from Glasgow .. a Gentleman of great respectability, a fancy gauze merchant of Paisley, waiting our arrival at the Inn .. we availed ourselves of their kind invitation to dinner after taking a glass of wine and a little Bride Cake (they being lately married) the Gentleman took us to see the different manufactorys and what curiousitys their was but their was very little except the sounding Ile attached to the old Abbey where we saw Queen Mary the mother of Robert, King of Scotland ..we then returned and dined from a very sumptuous dinner provided by our friendly host .. so ended this day Friday.

Saturday 18th Staid at home all day. Whent to Mrs... to tea, a party of about 20 Ladies and Gentlemen. Their the young people danced several country and Scottish reels. Left at 1/4 past 11 o'clock. So ends this day...very pleasant society.

Nov. Staid at home...Had several visitors Eliza sat the 3rd time to the painter...whent in the evening to Mr Graham...Mr & Mrs Fleming, an American Merchant, both of which played the piano very well... They had several dances Scotch reels, Shetspeys etc. The Company broke up at 11 o'clock. We staid to supper and left at 12 o'clock in a Noddy...So ends this day.

Nov 21st Staid at home. Visitors...Eliza and Celia sat to the painter. Whent to tea at Mr Stuarts ... Miss Cochrane played at the piano accompanied by Mr Stuart with the double flagelot. Had several dances... So ends this day.

Nov 22nd. This morning breakfasted with Mr Walter Wood. Met there Dr & Mrs Chalmers, Mr Irvin, Mr Pratt, a Lieut. in the Army... and another young gentleman. Had a little conversation about indifferent matters... After took a walk to the observatory. Saw their Camera Obscura and the magnifying glass magnified 1400 times... several visitors... Mr Scott Mr Cochrane and sister came to take C & E out walking. We whent to see the Panorama of the Battle of Waterloo...

Thursd. 23rd I sat this day for the painter... Eliza and Celia went to tea to Mrs Chartres had a great party and kept up dancing till 3 o'clock in the morning.

Nov 24th I sat to the painter... Capt.Wood called took out the young ladies.

Nov. 25th Celia, myself... whent to Mr john Flemings to tea... Cards was introduced played a short time as Dancing seemed the most wished for. After the Dancing was over a very splendid supper was sat down to where several toasts were given... healths named my family in N.S.Wales was drank. Broke up at 11.

Mon 27th Took a coach and whent to Hamilton... 10 miles from Glasgow... Was shown the Duke of Hamilton's Place where we saw a most grand collection of paintings by Reubens and others amongst them was Daniel in the Lions Den one of the most striking pieces I ever saw. There was also King George the Third and Queen Charlotte on each side of the throne which we ascended and sat down on. There was also a painting of Bonaparte which was done from the original. It was said to be a great likeness.

Nov 29 Whent to see Mrs Grants to a ball in the evening there being a great spirit for dancing 40 couples. I took a few hands of whist... did not break up till 3... Expect company tonight to bid us farewell. Celia sat the last time to finish her likeness.

Nov. 30th Left Glasgow at 11 o'clock for Edinburgh in the Coach. Changed horses at a small village called Cumbernaud. went as far as Gieryama in the Coach where a boat was in readiness to put us on board the Steamboat tug. Arrived at Newhaven about 6 o'clock in the evening. Took coach from there to Edinburgh being three miles. Arrived at Edinburgh half after 7 o'clock Expences being Two pounds Eighteen shillings and sixpence.

Fri. Dec 1st Took a walk around the town. Saw the castle, gaol... College and several buildings... At night whent to the theatre and saw performed the Tragedy of Douglas, after piece the Vampire...

Dec 2 Mr Hope took us out walking... Each took a basin of hare soup for which the charge 10d a basin... Called on Mrs Robinson... found her very pleasant woman and her two daughters. Had a little conversation concerning the schools in Edinburgh. She recommended me to a Miss Duncan. Whent to the Pantheon, saw there great horsemanship by Mr Clarke and others. Also the play the Antiquary after the piece The way To Win A Husband...

Monday 4th, Mrs Robinson and her daughter called on us to take me to Miss Duncan, the Boarding School Governess who lives in Picardy Place. A most delightful and airy situation. I agreed with her for one year only on account of Eliza's bad health but to continue longer if her health improves well at Fifty Two Pounds Ten Shillings per annum for board and lodgings , tuition in different branches about twenty Pounds more for each young lady...

Dec 5th Came home and was busy cutting out the of flannels... and getting everything ready for them to go to school tomorrow.

Dec 7th Called at Miss Duncan's to see how my daughter was. Found them rather poorly owing to sleeping in a strange bed and being up sooner than usual However they was taking a lesson in drawing, being their first attempt .. We sat down to dinner at half past four... The coach came to the door for us... we left the two young people at the school.

Fri 8th... took leave of my daughters... Arrived at Preston the next at half past 7 o'clock being the 9th.

Monday 11th visited the houses in Salford.

Dec 12th Left Blackburn at 2 o'clock. Arrived there at 1/2 before 2. Arrived Manchester half past 5 o'clock in company with Mr Thomas Brown my cousin.

Came to Mr Hargreaves another cousin where I promised to stay a month…
Dreamt my sister was dead.

Dec 15th Friday Mr Hargreaves and I called on Mr & Mrs Marsden. She also
took me to a manufacturing warehouse, Mr Heathcote's, where I bought a
piece of calico measuring 41 yards at 1/-…

Dec 17th. Sunday 17th Staid at home all day. Had company to tea and supper,
Mr & Mrs Browns Uncle to Mr Hargreaves… Broke up at 10 o'c.

Dec 18th… Recd a letter from Mr Jones with two enclosed .. and one from Mr
Watson's sister in Sydney. Whent to the play and saw 'Othello' performed
after piece '3 Weeks after Marriage'.

Dec 19th. Mr & Mrs Hargreaves and myself went to the man who is doing
my carriage to desire him to have it done this week…

22nd Dec. Friday 22nd. Dec set out for Bury. Mr hargreaves has taken me in
his Gig to a place called Openshawfolie where I had found my old nurse
and her husband who was both so gratified they hardly knew how to contain
themselves with joy, the old lady said she was sure she could not have rested
in her grave had she not seen me. They said they was both in her eighty first
year of their age and both looked as if they should live 20 years longer. We
went to Bury about a mile further where we put up at the Grey Mare, an Inn
about 20 yards from where my mother lived in the wild (circus, circular
drive) but all those houses had pulled down to make improvements to the
Church. Mr Hargreaves and I took a walk around the town. There was at
time a show of wild Beast to be seen, we whent in and was highly gratified
at the sagacity of the elephant. We dined at the Inn… Mr Hargreaves and I
whent to the old Church at Bury to procure the certificate of my age. The
clerk and I looked through the Register Book of parchment and I discerned
it first. I was born in the year of our Lord 1777, May 12 and christened 29th

Dec 23rd. Mrs Hargreaves and I whent to Market it being so near Christmas.
A very throng Market it was, so much so, that we lost each other. Called to see
if the carriage was finished.

Monday 25th Being Christmas day dined at home. Had no company. Mr & Mrs Hargreaves and I took a walk. Came home, had tea and read a few passages in the Scriptures.

Wed 27th. Whent to see if my carriage was finished, being Christmas the workmen were away.

Thurs 28th. Whent to see my Nephew, Thomas Foster, name of the place is Albion Street No. 12 Salford. He had alittle son home since last I saw him, about 10 weeks old and a very fine child he was.

Dec 29th Recd. letter... from my daughters. Whent to see if the carriage was packed up. Said it should be finished tommorrow. Staid at home all day after being ill of a cold.

Sun 31st. Continued to be very poorly. Mr Buchanan brought me news of the ship 'Malabar' having arrived from New South Wales.

Mon. Jan 1st 1821. Still confined to my room. Mr & Mrs Hargreaves paying attention to me. My old nurse and her husband came over from Bury to see me. Mrs Hargreaves gave them a bed and every comfort that they required after so long a walk for two old people in their eighty one years. They hardly knew how to express their joy at being able to see me before they died, a more venerable and better looking old man I never saw and a more healthy old woman at her age indeed she looked to live twenty or thirty years more..

Tues. 2nd. They set off home again, Mrs Hargreaves packing them up some mince pies and a little wine and water and I giving them a few shillings to asist them by the way. They left me with a heavy heart...

Sun 14th Jan.1821, This day the carriage whent by Baches, the carrier, for London.

Sun.28th Jan. took coach for Blackburn... Slept at Mr Brown's, dreamd Thomas came to Engalnd and that he said my little Betsy was very ill and subject to fits.

Mon.29th. Sold my houses for Three Hundred Pounds.

Weds.31st Came over to Blackburn... Found a letter from Mr Jones ...

Signed over my right to the houses in Salford and recd Three Hundred Pounds for them, being a loser of one Hundred Pounds.

Feb.1st. To Manchester ... to bid them goodbye.

Mon.5th Feb. Packing up this day. Whent to see Mr Hope's warehouse and looked at some cambric and callico. gave him an order for 100 pieces paid him in cash Eight Pounds for money laid down by him for me .. Bank of England No. 28578, 28586.

Tues.6th Feb. Took coach for London paid Three Pounds Three Shillings. My cousin John Hope and his wife and Thos. Foster dined with us at Mr Hargreaves. They all came to see me off in the coach for London. We started at two o'clock in the day. Settled with Mr Hargreaves for cash for me by him. Bothe him and Mrs Hargreaves behaved uncommon kind during my stay. There they wished me to stop another month or two Mrs Hargreaves made my two daughters , Jane & Elizabeth at home in Tasmania a present of two books. Mrs Hargreaves made me a present of a book of prayers named Nelsons Festivals and also the medicines both Eliza and I took.

Wed.7th. All this day in the coach and all the previous evening. We arrived at the White Horse Fetter Lane (*nearby St Pauls Cathedral)* before 7. I ingaged a bed. Capt. Dagg of the ship TUCAN called and told me he had seen James & George very well. Made me easy. Took a walk in the Cheapside and down Ludgate Hill... He (Mr Jones) gave me news of the Tucan arriving... no letters for me which made me very uneasy all day. Whent to Capt. Watson. Took lodging there . At night went as far as Capt. Atkinsons. He was just reading a letter from his son which he had got out of Mr Berry's box and he saw a packet directed to me but the Officer in Charge would not let them be taken as they must go throught the Post Office.

Feb.9th Mr Jones & I whent to Mr Berry's lodgings, No 8 Size Lane back of the Mansion House. He was not within but we left a note on his table to send my packet as soon as he got it which was to be within the afternoon, expences of it was 12/- and the Porter 2/-. I stopd up till after 12 o'clock reading them.

Mon.12th. Whent to the City called on Mr jones had a little conversation with him concerning going out to N.S.W and about the affairs of the Colony. Recd a packet of letters from my sister going through Manchester. Double postage on them 10/- expence.

Wed 14th Capt Watson whent on board the ship BRIXTON which was lying at the London dock, to look at the accommodation. Found them very good but could get no decisive answer, the broker not there. I purchased this day 1 doz. of Bell buttons, 1 pr. silver salts, 4 salt spoons, 1 doz. sugar stand, 7 table spoons, 18 teaspoons, 1 child's Coral, 1 silver eye glass, 4 ridicule clasps... 19 chairs, 5 yards of sarsenet & 7/6 for a gown and lost it going home. Also a pair of chandelier candlesticks...

Fri.16th Called on Capt. McIntosh who lives on Ratcliffe Highway. He had purchased a ship called the HOPE and intending to take passengers to N.S.W. He called a coach and we whent on board, she lying in the Canal refitting but she appears to be longer before she will sail than I wish to stop. I can make no agreement. The other half owner Degraves being on board. He also is going out with his small family to settle in Van Dieman's Land and wished for all the information I could give them which I did to the best of my judgement. Capt. McIntosh is quite the gentlemen. We all walked back calling in our way at a pastry cooks shop and taking refreshment. We parted and each party whent their own way after they giving me an invitation to dine.

Sat. 17th Whent to the City with a Mr Davison, a porter to purchase a desk but there was no one to suit me. He took me through the Mansion House, Guildhall and The Bank.

Feb.19th Removed to my new lodgings in Postern Row, No 9 Mr Sharp, Watchmaker at 16/- per week to find coals myself. After whent on board the MARINER sloop lying in the Limehouse Canal. The two owners called on me to enquire about the affairs of V. Dieman's Land and Port Jackson.

FRi.23rd.Feb. Whent to Moore Lane the Baches the carrier to send a small box to Manchester to Mr Hargreaves... Mr Jones called on me to advise me about what ship I must take. The owner of the MARINER called at night and we agreed...

Sat 24th. This day walked to the west end of the town as far as Grosvenor Street, the residence of Sir Robert Peel but was down in Staffordshire. Bought a canteen this day for George and 45 vols. of the British Essqyist and Gibbons History of Rome, 12 vols, from its foundation.

Tues.27th. Bought this day 12 setts of table matts, 12 doz doyleys... Gave an order for a quantity of cutlery ..

Wed.28th. Staid at home all day it freezing and snowing all day. The ditch round the Tower was frozen over and the boys were skating, my window being opposite I had full view of them. This day had in 250 cakes of Windsor soap.

Thurs.1st. At home all day. In the evening whent to see the Queen go to the Mansion House to be present for the benefit of some poor Society, but did not see her. She whent in a private entrance contrary to all expectations.

Fri.2nd Mar. Took a walk in the City. Whent to Wiston & Herrit Office 37 Old Broad Street, to enquire about the MARINER... Gave Mr Davison an order for some crockery ware... very dirty weather...

Tues.6th. Very bad weather. Gave orders for some stationery. Purchased some Irish linens. A very bad cough on me.

Wed.7th. Took a walk into Aldgate, Broad Street and made me some little purchases...

Mar.9th Recd. two letters from Edinburg, one from my daughters... Wrote one in answer... Purchased Clarke's Family Bible.

13th Mar.Tues. Got home my miniature frames.

Wed.14th Mar. Whent to Wakemans the carrier to see about 3 cases with Irish & Calicoes. Ordered a double barrelled fowling piece for George Bought the Incyclopedia Britanica, 20 vols, 30 guineas.

Thurs.15. Whent on board the MARINER... Whent to the theatre, the Royality, a very miserable performance.

16th.Mar.Fri… a L:ieut. Thomson, relation of Dr Chalmers called, brought me a note from my daughter Celia.

Sat 17th,… recd. a letter from D.Hope saying my daughters would be in town if the wind was fair today or tomorrow.

NOTE: GAP OF 20 DAYS.

Fri 6th. Whent to the Brokers of the MARINER to see when I could take my things on board. Mr Atkinson and I went to the City Canal. Came home in a waterman's boat. Bought a piece of Irish linen. Gave a woman 10 chemise to make and she has got the stay maker. Brought home 4 pr. stays.

Sat.7th April Whent to Mark Lane to Buckles, Bagsters & Buchanan to inquire concerning Rebecca's pension but got no answer… Lieut. Thompson called/..

Wed.11th. Whent on board the MARINER but no appearance of being ready.

Fri.13th Whent to Buckles Bay and Buchcanan, Mark Lane 33, to enquire about Rebecca's pension but got no more information than last Sat. Off to Whitehall to get the proper forms made out but called to see William Charles Wentworth. Staid with him too long till it was too late to go.

Sat.14th. Called on Mr Wm Wentworth… Whent to Whitehall the Admiralty & Army Pay Office to inquire about Rebecca's pension.

   Gained all I could after being referred from one to another till I was tired. Got the necessary forms from them…

Tues.17th. Purchased a trunk this morning, gave 21/- for it. Celia & Eliza gone to order their pelisses & pay the Doctor's bill Five Pounds Twelve Shillings.

Apr.18th.Wed. Whent to Broad street 53… ordered from Cooper & Eliot some looking glasses, a sofa, A Mohogany Dressing & writing case. Packed up all my luggage…

Apr.21st. Sat. Got my goods on board the MARINER.

Apr.22nd. Whent to the Foundling Hospital a beautiful litle chaple and a most gratifying sight to see such a number of little females in such good order and an equal number of boys...

Apr.25th. Whent on board . Nothing doing. mr Williams and I Whent to Clementinas to look at a piano.

Thurs.26th Mr Thomson called on us and we whent to Greenwhich Hospital by water... saw through the painted Hall and chaple. Came home by coach. Mr T. spent the evening with us.

Apr.27th. Whent on board the ship. Am afraid she will not sail this three weeks yet.

Sun.29th. Whent to a Scotch church in Miles Lane... Mr Thomson called and took us.

Apr.30th Whent on board the MARINER, Nothing doing...

May 1st. Was taken very ill of my old complaint on the lungs...

Thurs.3rd. Eliza & I whent on board the MARINER. Still very ill. Was obliged to go to bed. Mr Thomson brought two tickets of the speaking of the Bible Society at the King's Concert Rooms, Haymarket. Only Eliza and Mr Thomson went, Celia staying at home with me on acct of me being so ill.

Sun.6th. Called in a physician, Dr Frampton on this day. Gave his opinion to Dr White.

Sat.May 12th... this being my birthday 44 years of age, my complaint began to take a favourable turn.

Sun 15th. Celia & Eliza whent to dine at Mr Ross a little way out of town, accompanied by Mr Hope and Mr Thomson...

Fri.May 18th. Celia and Mrs Hope going to Manchester. They left the Swan with two necks in the regulater...

May 19th... sent the last of my luggage on board, Mr Thomson and Eliza going on board the MARINER.

Sun.20th Staid at my lodgings, Mr Thomson took out Eliza awalking in the afternoon.

Tues.22nd. Took coach for Gravesend where we arrived about 5 o'clock in the afternoon... We staid all night at the Inn PRINCE OF ORANGE. Mr Thomson went in quest of lodgings. I thought it best to go there for the good of my health.

May 23rd. Took lodgings at Mr Beers, Pilot, Lower Terrace at 50/- per week with the servants attendance, boarding ourselves...

Sat. May 26th. Mr Thomson and I whent amarketing. Mr & Mrs Dunn, passengers in the MARINER... called on us , they having been down at Gravesend 7 months waiting for a ship...

Wed,30th. Whent to market... few things to sell only purchased a few eggs and butter... Mr & Mrs Dunn... took tea with us... Had a few games of whist.

Thurs.31st. Mr Dunn called to know if I had any commands to London as he was going down to settle some misunderstanding with the Brokers of the MARINER, Witson & Hewitt...

June 3rd... Ship LUSITANIA came down to Gravesend ready to clear out.

June Mon.4th Nothing to do. Mr & Mrs Dunn called and we went out walking to a very pleasnt place situate on the River Thames, a bathing House, a small park adjoining it. There are seats for visitors and where you have most beautiful view of shipping sailing to & from London.

June 5th. Mr.D. ..to London.. We hear by advertisement in the Times paper the MARINER is to be down on Sunday next. LUSITANIA sailed from Gravesend.

June. Wed.6th. I think this will now compleat my twelve months in England as we landed at Portsmouth on 21st. June 1820. I am very afraid we shall not sail for that place before the Day. Recd. a letter from Mr Atkinson requesting me to come to London to put my cabin in order... Accordingly Mr Thomson and I set off 2 mins to 1 o'clock and arrived at the Dundee Arms at 1/4 to 5 o'clock. We immediately whent on board the MARINER. It came on to rain very hard and everyone had done work on board for the day we could not do anything that afternoon...Walked to Mr A. where they kindly received me and I slept there all night, Mr.T. going to his lodgings. Recd. a letter from Celia from Manchester. All very well.

June Thurs.7th. this day Mr Atkinson & I whent on board the MARINER and made a a great clearance... and put out of the cabin... trunks nos. 7,9,15,16, & 20. and 1 small bale, 1 box of Mrs Kemps marked 21 down in the hold as owners had charged freight on them... I slept there that night as did also Mr Thomson. Had they been related to me they could not have been more kind.

June Fri.9th... this day came down to Gravesend... Mr Thomson and Eliza took a walk to see Mr & Mrs Dunn...

Wed.13th. No ship or signs of it ..

Thurs.June 14th. Mr Cox (another passenger) came down this evening and brought the news that the MARINER could not proceed on her voyage for want of means. He also brought a letter from Mr Jones... advising passengers to seek redress... They in consequence are going to London tomorrow morning viz Mr Dunn, Cox and Thomson to join Major Homen in complaints to the Lord Mayor. Now this is ever since 1st of april when he first ingaged that the ship should sail, I have been living at very heavy expence and in consequence my sickness has increased it and God only knows now when we shall get off, but I will put my trust in Him who alone can judge.

June Sat.16th This morning recd. two letters from Celia and one for Eliza and one for myself, wishing to go back with me in consequnce I wrote her an answer to come up immediately. The Gentlemen all returned with the news that the ship was to be down on Tuesaday.

June Wed.20th. This evening the MARINER came down to Gravesend.

June 21st Thurs. Whent on board the MARINER. Had some little dispute about getting into my cabin.

June 22nd. Fri. Mr Atkinson came down from London and brought my daughter Celia with him. I returned with him to settle about her passage. Slept at Mr.A.

June 24/25/26 all deal with disputed passages.

Sun 26th We weighed anchor and sailed from Gravesend. Whent down the River about 14 miles was obliged to come down to anchor owing to the wind being foul. Most of the ladies were a little sick owing to the motion of the ship.

June Wed 27th. 1/4 past 11 o'clock in the morning weighed anchor and got under weigh. Very light wind and rather heavy sea. Most of the ladies very sick.

Fri.29. The Pilot left us. Passed Dover this morning.

Sat.30th Foul winds and beating to get to Portsmouth. Anchored at Ride on the Isle of Wight .. Some went on shore, took lodgings at 3/- per day while on shore.

July 2nd. Rained all day could not go on shore… went on shore at Portsmouth, found Capt. in difficulties in regard to provisions on the ship. Heard the owner was in gaol. The passengers were obliged to consent paying for their provisions…

Thurs.5th July. This day the gentlemen went on shore and bought the remainder of the provisions… Had to open the Hatch to get their dollars to pay for it. Sailed from Ride this evening with a foul wind…

This is the last entry with its intermittent remarks, in Mary's small note book. N.I.

Letter 3

*W*ritten in England from Mary Reibey

London feby7 14th 1821.
Our traveller is now as busy as today's tourists, buying up all the fallals, the decorative goods not readily obtainable in Sydney town. The advertisements which later appear in the Sydney Gazette repeat these goods for sale from

> ribbons, silks, Bombazeens to black Nails of different sorts... and shoes.

Plaids from Kilmarnock, she orders, each to be clearly labelled.with the appropriate clan.no less than 200 yards. Sydney probably celebrated Burns even then.

The letter may indicate that Mary originally meant her two young ladies to return home with her to New South Wales contrary to her private notes.(Ante).Again from this letter we realise the difficulty of finding passage to New South Wales in 1821 . The cost of the fares, the charge to bring back the fabulous carriage and all her 20 chests, her packing cases, her purchases sre closely examined in this letter to her Cousin David Hope.

Thomas Mackdougall Brisbane became Governor of NSW in early December 1821, having arrived in NSW in November 1821, travelling more or less at the same time as the Reibey family in (another vessel) Mariner.

Mary's desire to speak with Thomas Brisbane is connected with her claim from the Government for recompense for the loss of her coal carrying clipper "Eclipse." While loading coal at Newcastle in 1818 this Reibey coal and timber clipper was spirited away by the convict workers, manipulating long boats and sails to get the clipper out through Nobby's heads and apparently manipulating the soldiers on guard to ignore the escape. Eclipse was never heard of again. The Government was responsible for its workers.

Mr Throsby. ie surgeon, explorer Charles Throsby of Newcastle and Camden district. had discovered land, as Mary writes;

> there has been a very fine track of Land lately discovered by Mr Throsby…

She refers to his possibly last venture over the pass between the south coast and Goulburn. Mary Reibey settled her Thomson family on the rich pastures of the Illawarra district, obtaining grants on the Shoalhaven, a property named Illaroo. Thomsons still farm the land at Illaroo and elsewhere on the south coast. Her affectionate ending to the letter shows how the young legal cousin David Hope has now become a close member of her family.

From Mary Reibey whilst shopping in London
to her cousin David Hope, at 66 Brunswick Street, GLASGOW

London, feby 14th 1821.
From 22 Suffolk street Commercial Road, London

My Dear Cousin,

You will excuse me not answering your letter of the 2nd feby as I have been so taken up with business, their has been a ship calld the Tuscan arrivd from Sydney lately which I got letters by from my family and which I had a difficulty in finding them out as the Come in a private box so that it took me nearly Three days before I could get them, you may think my anxiety / however I got very pleasant news they were all very well and happy and has they say they happiness whould be Complete if I near them, I have on this day been on board the Brixton laying in the London Docks with a friend of mine to agree about my passage out but the Captain was not on board therefore I have not yet agreed but I shall tomorrow as the accomadation seems very good / she is expected to sail in a month from this date which you see I Shall not have much time to to spare / I wrote my daughters on the 10th so I expect an answer by friday next -they had a wish to, stay another three months but that they will not be able / but they shall stop their till I go which giving them time to come up to London will be three weeks or a month more as perhaps the ship may not sail by a week so soon as expected but they was to sail the 28th this month / I will thank you to purchase me about 200 yards of different pattern plaids from Kilmarnock, 50 yards of each pattern / let them be good and as Cheap as you can that I know I have no occasion to warn you of and let their be attached to each pattern the Clan they are of, you will know how to send them to me better than I can tell you, direct for me at Mr Jones 53 old broad street, and Draw for the amount on him- I should like you when my daughters are Comeing of for London if you had any Business in Eding to see them of in the best smack their and has comfortable as possible but I should not wish you to go over on purpose /as Mr Nash I daresay will be kind enough on your account to do that you may let Capt Wood know of this Conveyance / perhaps he might avail himself of it / Cabin passenger 80 guineas Steerage 40 dltto and Mr Scott, he wished me to say what may be good to send out their / I really cannot tell him now as the place is so glutted with goods I shall not take out myself anything like what I intended /they asked me 30 pounds to take out the Carriage I have not yet agreed with them to do so has I think it too much/ Your letter of advice came too late about the Houses as I sold them for £300, when I left Manchester I desired John to write you which I suppose he did/ I am now so busy in making my purchases and London is so large a place it takes me nearly all day to walk from one place to another- I was very proud to hear your account of my daughters being so very well in health / I can assure you it added to my recovery, I am extremely obbliged to you for the attention you have paid to them on every occasion,and the Interest you have taken in procuring me letters of introduction to the Commissanys brothers but I have not yet read them, Mr Thomas Brishan is expected in London every day, I should like if you could procure me amongst your friends a letter or two of introduction to him / I understand he does not expect to sail from Greenock as the owners of the ship he wished to go in and he disagreed, / you was kind enough to say you whould send me a few apples for which I was much obblid but I was obliged to leave for London- you may tell Mr Scott that Irish Linins, hucaback lining silk Books of different kinds , Morsellas super fine broad Cloth & black nails of different sorts and Steel Cutting and (shoes womens) and sundry other articles which I cannot enumerate these are such as I should take out but it is intirely a risk now as their is such an abundance gone out their / their has been a very fine track of Land lately dlscovd by Mr Throsby the person you may recolect that found the last Track out some hundreds of Thousands acres without a tree and very rich land /it is supposed it will be fine Country I cannot be as explanitory as I whould wish now Has I have a friend waiting to go out with me now, but I hope you will course,you have an opportunity of letting my daughters know of any part of this letter you may think is nessery - give my respects to all Inquireing friends I am afraid you will hardly make this out but I know you will excuse my Errors I hope Mary is; well / I am my dear Cousin

yours affectionately
M.Reibey.

Letter 4

A Letter from Son James to The Scottish cousin, David Hope a broker in Glasgow. Mary, obviously, has 'stirred the possum' amongst her family. Cousin David Hope has sent Gazettes and letters to distant VDL.In return James,from Hobart, writes to his cousin perhaps for the first time;

> I hope we shall not be such strangers as we have been for so many years

and proceeds to detail the family. He then answers the many questions which have been put by the curious Scot...answers which add to our picture now of the Colony as James knew it in 1821.The letter, mailed in Hobart on May 6th 1821,when his mother and sisters were impatiently awaiting the Mariner to pick them up at Gravesend, was delivered in Glasgow 7 months later ,on 21 December 1821. Such a slow pace of life, one notes, left plenty of time for decision making. James mentions the fraud perpetrated at the bank at which young brother George has been employed. Van Diemens Land Bank was founded in 1823. There were apparently some private banking institutions. The executions of six men refer to the clamping down by the authorities on the bushrangers of those years.Van Diemens Land was over run by desperate men, mostly escaped convicts. To survive they plundered and murdered amongst the sparse settlements. James also happily tells of the profitable export trade in wool, wheat potatoes... all this by 1821. The VDL colony was a mere 15 years of age. Parson Knopwood figures in most contemporary reports as a fox hunting parson. John West gently writes;

> The gayety of his *(Rev Knopwood)* disposition made him a pleasant companion and a general favourite, yeoix Tan tivvy tan tivvy!.

Port Dalrymple, (Launceston) is quite a journey down through the middle of Tasmania and this journey of course was made by carriage and horse.. Interesting that James had collected his two young sisters from Entally, Jane -Penelope and Elizabeth to settle them in a Hobart School... It seems that James has not met David Hope. Therefore there is a question mark over his, James' possible earlier visit to England.One thing is sure; from the excellence of this letter (in the original) James has been well schooled in more than the 3 Rs.

From son James in Hobart, to Cousin David Hope, Broker, Glasgow.Postage paid to London, a Portsmouth Ship Letter Letter received in Glasgow 21 December 1821.

Hobart Town, Van Diemens Land , May 6th,1821.

Dear Cousin,

I beg to acknowledge the Receipt of a Letter from you to my Mother per Skelton, and was very happy to hear you where well.

I hope we shall not be such strangers as we have been for so many years. The manner in which my Mother always mentioned with you and your Brothers and Sister I was always Lead to Respect you. I sincerely hope this will find you well. My Brother Thomas to whom I sent your letter promised to write to you . He is the Eldest and Twenty Five old to Day. He is married and one Little Girl as I suppose Mother has informed you of. I have been Married these Five Years but have no Family. My Brother George who was in the Bank has now left it, in Consequence of it nearly failing and they could not keep up such an Establishment. The Cashier had lent all the money out long before my Brother joined but was not found out till lately. He had lent £12,000 to a set of Rascalls who Refused to pay it back to him again knowing He could not make a noise about it, so in fact the Bank had Existed for nearly 3 years Entirely upon the Public Confidence,but I will give you a part of his own letter to me on the Subject which I enclose, The Westmorland arrived here yesterday I Received the Gazettes you were kind enough to send me together with your Letter of Recommendation in favour of Captain Potton. I enclose you some of our Hobart Gazettes, for your Perusal, /last week Ten Unhappy Men Suffered the Sentence of the Law which you will see by the Gazette / The most awfull Sight that was ever Witnessed on this Island . There Never was above 5 people Executed here since the Colony was Established.

You wish to know if there is not something suitable in the way of Produce to send to you. The only Produce New South Wales Exports is Wool which goes to London, about two Ships Cargoes a year, / we export very Little Wool from this Island , it being very Coarse , at Present, altho People are now paying more attention to it than they Did. Wheat we export to Sydney about 50 or 60 Thousand Bushells every year with a Large Quantity of Potatoes . You wish to know the State of Religion in these Colonies . you must know that before the Administration of Govr. Mc Quarie There was so little attention paid to these Colonies that we hardly ever had a Clergyman in Sydney but There is now at Present 4 or 5 in Sydney, one Here that Came out when this Island *(TAS)* was first Colonised *(1804)* and one at Port Dalrymple who has been there about a year, but both of these Latter Gentlemen I cannot speak of in Flattering Termes. Mr Knopwood who is here has been Regularly brought up to the Church of England, but having Run thro a fortune at Home *(UK)*,was fain to Accept a Situation out here to Accompany our first Govr. Collins. He is a Very Profane Man and had been what is Commonly Called a Fox Hunting Parson. / The other Gentleman Formally was a Missionary out here but went Home and got ordained. I cannot speak anything in favour of his Abilities or Oratory.There is now a Number of Gentlemen of the Vessylian Persuasion in Sydney who have Erected Chapels and I believe have been a Great Acquisition there in Reward to forwarding the Cause of Morality.

You will be pleased to excuse the Shortness of this letter as I have only been in from Port Dalrymple two days a Distance of 126 miles by land to fetch my two Youngest Sisters to go to Schools / I am still very Tired and then the vessell sails at Daylight in the Morning . Namely Regalia Captn Dixon. I have not wrote to my Mother alas I suppose ere this they have left Your Shores for Australia since June / my Wife and two little Sisters Desire their Best Respects to you Hoping you will not fail writing me by every opertunity as I shall not fail to do so.

I Remain Dear Cousin

Yours Very Truly

James H. Reibey.

Letter 5

From George Reibey to Cousin David Hope in Glasgow.

And surely, this letter from George is a splendid example of a contemporary's tale of what for me are the exciting titbits of Colonial history. George was still living at his mother's Sydney residence in 1821 awaiting news of the travellers' return. Mary Reibey and daughter Eliza are settling themselves into lodgings at Gravesend, attended by the ever present suitor, Lieut. Thomson; they await the much delayed Mariner. Date May 29th 1821. George is more than expert in the composition and presentation of a Victorian age letter; he is, at twenty, very well informed, very observant. No wonder there was so much grief in 1823 when this young son died. In the Travel Notes, during this holiday in the U.K. Mary noted;

> Sat.24th (March) Bought a canteen for George and 45 Vols of the British Essqyist (sic) and Gibbons History of Rome 12 vols from its foundation.

George, I believe, makes sincere obeisance to his God in his tribute to his mother and family. His vivid description of the conditions of the Colony must add of course to the picture presumably already given to his cousins by the travellers. No regular Mail from either Launceston or Hobart (to the U.K.), letters will be forwarded through Sydney friends. In London Loyds acts as American Express Offices do today... poste restante. He notes a circumstance

> of the greatest importance is 'Distillation' permission for which has recently been recently granted by the British Governt. to the Colonies.

Goodbye to the sly grog trade, the illicit stills... He highlights the hopes for the new settlement at Port Macquarie, for the growth and 'exportation' of sugar cane. The expected fall out from Commissioner Bigge's Enquiry is a matter of major discussion amongst the Colonists, whether a certain Party

> whose sole object is their own aggrandisement with the depression of those who have once been prisoners, without any reason to their real Interests of the Colonies.that class of People being not only the most numerous but the most opulent...

As is evident George is writing of the emancipists; did he know of his mother's status? Most likely not..For Mary Reibey was surely an Emancipist: I believe well disguised by her piety, i.e. her participation in Good Causes and her clever management of business . Another family mystery is the complete absence of any visit to any people called Reibey during this 1820 visit to the U.K. The name never features. For me this is explained by the Calcutta connection. (See "Mary Reibey—Molly Incognita") Yet George anxiously writes of a Heydock... Laws connection ,vide:

> I have frequently when here heard my Mother speak of Relations named Hargreaves but forbears mentioning them in any of Her Letters since her arrival in England, I am quite at loss what to attribute it to ..

In her travel notes Mary does in fact speak very affectionately of the Hargreaves. (pp 32). Finally this letter is obviously a first attempt at establishing a written connection with cousin David Hope. What of the intervening years at least since 1818 ?

From George Reibey, Mary's son, of Sydney to Cousin David Hope named as Merchant of Glasgow. Rcd 29th Nov 1821. per Skelton, Captn Dixon.

NOTE: FOLLOWING AFTER THE INTERMINABLE VICTORIAN EXPRESSIONS OF GRATITUDE, GEORGE'S LETTER HAS SOME INTERESTING SNIPPETS EG THE INTRODUCTION OF LEGAL DISTILLATION, SETTLEMENT AT PORT MACQUARIE TO GROW SUGAR CANE, HIS VIEWS OF THE BIGGE REPORT: OUR TWENTIETH CENTURY EAR FORGIVES HIM.

New South Wales , Sydney May 29th 1821.

My Dear Sir

It is the request of a very Dear Mother, and sincere wish of my affectionate Sisters that I should address you but beg firstly to introduce myself as George, the youngest Son of your Cousin Mrs M Reibey and as such put forth a claim (Tho' but slight) to your friendship - but do not suppose this arises merely from a submission to the will of a Parent, or an acquiescence to the wishes of my Sisters, No Sir—receive it as a tribute of gratitude offered by the loving Son of Her to whom you showed so much kindness and attention - Nothing be assured calls forth sooner as kindness shown to Her , the unfeigned sentiments of esteem or grateful feeling from the breast of any of the offspring of a Mother - whose long anxious and great exertion for the improvement and future happiness was scarcely ever surpassed.

In speaking of those we love, an enthusiasm often times caries us far beyond what the cool observing eye thinks due ; but these believe me are the genuine sentiments of a Heart impressed with a deep sence of gratitude to Him whose great mercy and kindness bestowed so sure a blessing in the Land of Depravity.-

Once again permit me to return not only my sincere thanks but those of all my Brothers and Sisters,to you,your Dr. Brother and Sister, and all your kind hearted friends for the very great kindness and unremitting attention bestowed upon Person so Dear to us all.

It is the intention of my Brothers Thos. & James to write to you all, it is out of their power to take advantage of this conveyance, both being residents of Van Diemens Land , one of Launceston the other of Hobart Town on opposite sides of the Island , there not being~ any regular Mail from either of these places they forward all letters for Europe through me which probably they may do before this Vessel sails.

A letter from my Sister Celia Date 26th Octor. at Glasgow when on a Visit to you came to hand on the 26th Inst. She says it was our Mother's purpose to leave England in about three Months from that Date - now therefore we are anxiously and hourly expecting Her.-

I forwarded a Paquet about 5 mos. since enclosed in one from a Mr Hollstonecraft a resident here to a Mr Berry a passenger by the Cockburn, but being simply Directed "Mrs Reibey" / I am apprehensive it did not reach Her as it is most probable He did not know what part of England She was in or how to dispose of it / if so In the event of such being the case, I beg you will have the goodness to learn what became of it, A letter left at Loyds will find the Gentleman.

I would have given you a description of our Country, its manner customs &c (which I presume might have been somewhat interesting) had not my Mother & Sisters got the start of me ./ one or two circumstances only worth mentioning have transpired since their departure among which the one of greatest importance is 'Distillation' permission for which has been recently granted by the British Governt .to the Colonies.-

(COOPERS DISTILLERY WAS SET UP AT BLACKWATTLE BAY, AT WHAT IS NOW THE JUNCTION OF PARRAMATTA RD. AND CITY ROAD BROADWAY)

A new Colony has lately been Planted at a place named Port McQuarie about two hunds. (miles) to the Northwards of Port Jackson Head Quarter, its foundation has for its object the cultivation of the sugar cane being much warmer than here/ the highest hopes are entertained of its success/ if such are realised , very great advantages by its means will accrue to the Country -an important Article for Exportation will be afforded which is much wanted,it will also detain in circulation a great portion of the Colonial Capital which is annually sent out for foreign produce,

Mr Commissioner Biggs sailed for England about three Mos. Past finished his Enquiry from the result of which Great Changes are expected,Public opinion differ widely as to their comnsequent tendency whether to the advantage or disadvantage of the Country,- one party draw their conclusion from his having from the time of his arrival attached himself to a certain Party existing here whose sole object is their own aggrandisement with the depression of those who have once been Prisoners, without any reason to their real Interests of the Colonies.

(I HAVE NOT FOUND ANY EVIDENCE YET TO SHOW THAT MARY'S FAMILY WAS AWARE OF HER STATUS AS AN EMANCIPIST. REMEMBERING HOW SKILLFULLY SHE DISGUISED HER COMING IN THE 1806 CENSUS AND LATER THE 1838 CENSUS. THIS COMMENT AROUSES SPECULATION.)

/ But cool reflection will show such can never happen, that class of People not only the most numerous but the most opulent,- neverless if an attempt of such a nature should be made it is not impossible that a second Washington might rise up among us -but by the bye as we are not yet independent perhaps such an expectation may be considered too much of Treason which we read of here is often punished with either an Axe or an Halter and speaking sincerely I should not much relish the performance of such an operation on my own Neck,/ But the English themselves I find by your News Papers take great liberties with their Rulers without molestation. and likely an unconscious or ignorant expression of an Australian Savage might be looked over for once/

I have frequently when here heard my Mother speak of Relations named Hargreaves but forbears mentioning them in any of Her Letters since her arrival in England .

(NOTE MARY WRITES OF HER VISIT TO THE HARGREAVES IN HER TRAVEL NOTES)

I am quite at loss what to attribute it to, whether to forgetfulness on her part or unkindness on theirs I hope there's no exception.

I shall feel great Interest in forming a correspondence with both you & Mr Jn. & Willm. Hope..should have written to them by this Vessel but I believe she does not touch any part of England/

If the Edinbourg Review could be sent out with convenience to yourself I should consider it as a great favouor if you could transmit it regularly. Conclude with being

My Dear Sir,

with great esteem,

Yours

Geo. Reibey.

Letter 6

𝒯his manuscript (from internal evidence) is an excerpt of a letter to James in Hobart from his brother George in Sydney Town. It was enclosed with a letter from James to Cousin Hope in Edinburgh in 1821. The two letters were "handed down," enfolded, to a descendant in Sherborne. Written prior to George's death in 1823 I date it at 1820-1821 since Mother is still away (in the U.K,) according to George, when discussing his money affairs in the letter.

Of interest to me is the personal relationship evident between the writer, George, and his brother James. The letter speaks volumes for the family life of Mary Reibey's children. At the very end of this letter George though only twenty years speaks as an older, canny business man about the trading Hint he has given to his brother

few thousands in a short time will pay well for the purpose of trading and buying up wheat...

Moreover the written expression reminds us again of the high standard of education available in the Colony at that time. George, now just twenty years of age, would have been schooled at least till 1817, we know that he had attended a Latin school,as his mother had written to the Hopes. See Letter 2, 12/8/1818.

Quite fascinating to read contemporary George's frank appraisal of the marriages ..western style, of two Aboriginal couples in Parramatta.

The women he writes;

broght up and civilised (sic) by the Native Institutions the former (men) lately Breeched for the occasion / Farm with Farming utensils &c is given them for the purpose of commencing the Business on a large scale

But significantly, though expressing his good wishes, George adds;

It's all a Bottle of smoke. They certainly are the most degenerate mortals on the Universe between them and the Brute Creation there scarcely is a step / in my opinion their Ideas will ever attain to more than the knowledge of a good belly full

In hindsight the irony of his remarks on the uncertainty of life is tragic. Shortly afterwards George was to die from the effects of an accident while tree felling at Entally House near Hadspen, VDL

Historical fact as written by contemporaries is always welcomed by historians; this letter gives us so many clues as for example, The dating of the expedition to Port Macquarie... the New Settlement... complete with prisoners and Soldiers, hopefully to cultivate sugar cane. The sealing industry was in full swing, having been an active and lucrative industry in the Pacific and Atlantic during the 19th century. Mary's sister Mrs Foster is not popular with the second generation;vide the paragraph about Rebecca's bonnets. Mrs. Forster was a dressmaker.

Despite Mary Reibey's strong annoyance (see Letter 8) re James' marriage to the young widow Rebecca Breedon the brothers have stood firm. George concludes;

with love to Rebecca , and am my dear Brother James your very loving and affecytionate Brother

Geo Reibey, Sydney.

This is the existing fragment of a letter from George Reibey to his brother James, undated but written prior to George's death in 1823. It appears to have been sent from Sydney; was found folded within Letter 5.

The letter begins:

will save them so much unhappiness, Miss Black and De Mestro were married a few days ago. they are now well paird. both being of the Pygmy race, but are, to use a common expression 'little and good.' He is in my opinion one of the most worthy little fellows in the Colony, Her amicable disposition is well known,

Two other marriages are to take place tomorrow at Parramatta which have causd. a great deal of Interest throughout the whole Colony, You would be a long time in guessing who the Parties are if I did not choose to tell you that they are two Pair of our Sable Countrymen and Women, the latter brought up and civilised by the Native Institutions, the former lately breeched for the occasion / Farm with Farming Utensils &c is given them for the purpose of commencing the Business on a large scale. They have my sincere wishes for their welfare and Prosperity / But still think a Man possessed even of my small share of foresight if asked His opinion on it might safely answer, It is all a Bottle of smoke / They certainly are the most degenerate Mortals in the universe between them and the Brute Creation there scarcely is a Step / in my opinion their Ideas will never attain to more than the knowledge of a good Belly full / your old Shipmate Miss Browne married to Brown of the Mary shortly before He left for India. Died of a short time back in Child Birth. I saw her the evening before in perfect health and spirits early next morning she was Dead, the uncertainty of Human Life never before made so great an impression on my mind by am not yet sufficiently methodised to expatiate on the awful visitation of God. / If this was from Geo. Allen this Subject would see the end of at least two or three Sheets having become almost a Rank Methodist / Three of four of the Government vessels are going off tomorrow for the New Settlement (Port McQuarie) laden with Prisoners and Soldiers under the command of Captn. Allemond of the 48th Regt. I believe they intend cultivating the Sugar Cane as the Climate is supposed to be very favourable for it.

Whyte and his wife saild three Days ago for Port Dalrymple, they intend I believe sealing there, He, I suppose join Messrs. Montgaux Whyte Read & Co.

You may tell Rebecca (JAMES' WIFE) not to expect Her Bonnetts by the Speeds, having heard Mrs. Foster (MARY R.'S SISTER) making frivolous excuses for not having them done, when they sent about them, and also say, as She had no sent up a Box for them, she would not do them / I mention with the view that the <u>great</u> <u>disappointment</u> if they do not come, may not be to sudden as probably it might affect her fine flow of Spirits / besides I wish to show her how ready and willing her <u>sincere</u> <u>friend</u> Mrs. Foster is to oblige her on <u>all</u> <u>occasions</u> -

Your old Friend Grimes arrivd. here a short time back from a most unsuccessful Sealing Voyage having procured but 800 and lost his Chief Officer and six Other of his men, / He saild. again three day ago for England by way of Otehete freighted by Marsden, He desired me to be sure and remember him to you. You say in one of your letters ,you enclosd.some certificates you must afterwards have changed your mind as I did not receive them. with regard to the money you owe me, not being in immediate want of it , I think I had better lay it out at interest until Mother arrives..(MARY RETURNED IN THE MIDDLE OF 1821) Hamilton & hughes return to England by the Shipley / they absolutely detest this place , but are extravagant in their praise of Hobart Town / they were not noticed here as much as they expected, Hamilton I believe writes to,you by their vessel-

You will receive a visit shortly from the commander in chief by the Midas,/ Mrs Lang (alias Mrs Underwood) and Dick go down also by Her for the purpose of trading and buying up Wheat in exchange -by the way do not forget the Hint I have given you touching the Wheat- a few thousands in a short time will pay well. The Gazettes from 13th of January up to the 10th inst.accompany this / I have written almost enough this time , therefore conclude with love to Rebecca , and am my dear Brother James

your very loving and

affectionate Brother

Geo Reibey Sydney

Letter 7

George Reibey to his cousin David Hope in Glasgow From Sydney /14th February, 1823.

Dated Sydney 14th February 1823 this bulletin is a full documentary... a most revealing communique. The young gentleman presents as a stiff, well bred, well informed and highly critical late 18th century model, yet right up to the (1823) minute as far as local politics are concerned. With hindsight I wonder at this family Mary R. so carefully fashioned . The internal evidence of this letter forces me to ponder anew whether and if the boy knew of his mother's emancipist status. He certainly argues cogently about the current Emancipist Debate, which is exacerbated by the newly released Bigge report. Since Mary Reibey later fudged the 1828 Census the secret possibly remained with her.. Would he have written so passionately about this contentious matter had he known? Historians will differ.

Friendly relations have been established between the distant cousins. Present day correspondents must find it rather mind boggling : events would be so out of date! All that time which elapsed between despatch and reception. George has received no less than two letters from Scotland , from cousin David, together with 8 Numbers (second hand) of the Edinburgh Revue; letters dated 28th December 1821 and 28th Feby. 1822.

Briefly skimming some salient points of his letter, for this opus is some 20 pages in length, it appears that George praises the "thrifty saving turn....the judious economy" of the used Review which Journal he admires.

He writes ; it

> exceld every other work of the Kind in Europe which led me to make choice of it in my first letter to you... my judgement is confined to Britain being pretty well read in most of her best Authors..(*George had a special penchant for the romantic novels of Sir Walter Scott.*)... through my Books I learn that France is a Nation deeply learned and far advanced in literature...

High praise from a distant yet well read Colonial, in the early 19th century, which belies much of the Francophobia that has been imputed to the English speaking world. It is refreshing to read of George's ready admission of the possible influence of the newspapers from which stems his declared admiration of the Wig (sic) faction. George quotes from Goldsmith's 8 vols. of popular science which was used for many years as a ready Reference. From Sydney in 1789, some 33 years earlier, Newton Fowell of the Sirius, wrote to his parents in Devon, suggesting they read Goldsmith's description of "the ostrich like the emu." George Reibey here mentions Goldsmith's self evident truth;

That life is a Book of which he whose observations have been confined to his own Native Country have only read a single page.

Ah yes! But of course they'd never experienced T.V.

The former Governor of the Colony, 1810 - 1822, Lachlan Macquarie receives due credit, Samuel Marsden is duly condemned, all with good reason according to George's summary of

the Leaders of this party (*emancipists*) between which and A Certain Set here a violent enemity and jealousy exists..the latter pride themselves upon having come free ... evince their contempt and dislike by the most arrogant demeanour...

He records the great 'indignation' protest meeting held in Sydney in 1820, where a very large £1000 was subscribed to send Eager and Redfern to appeal to the House of Commons. George adds an aside ;

... If you are not heavily sick, tired and impatient of my treatise upon colonial politicks you will read on...

More or less mesmerised the wise reader does just that of course.

And George continues in grand rhetoric to berate himself should his prejudging of the Bigge report's influence be incorrect, despite his belief in the colony's character of justice and moderation. He writes in even greater praise of Macquarie's splendid efforts to give emancipists their rightful freedom of ownership and proper place in the colonial free society. If all colonists with similar beliefs wrote so feelingly to their British relatives as has done Master George, then Macquarie, maybe unknowingly, received an overwhelming vote of support. The letter sweeps on in a grand flood of satire

... does he (*Macquarie*)... who has made so many of his fellow - men happy desire to be thought and spoken of with horror as the determined opponent of all good works ... the merciless persecutor of that paragon of holiness Saint Samuel (*Marsden*)

... were they... the good people of your country (Scotland) cooly to examine the portly carcase- round fat jolly red face and laughing eyes of the said Saint of ours whom ...they have been accustomed to view as the very type of mortification and woe with the pale emaciated visage and thin spare form etc etc..

George carries on about the profligacy of the missionaries without censure from Marsden

"it is a fact that one of them (*missionaries*) keeps several of the Native Women under the very eyes of his wife . Some credit,..to Mr Marsden if he had turned his attention to the spiritual way of our own Aborigines...

Despite the sometimes tedious length of this letter, it is undoubtedly an interesting exposé of the unrest and lively growth within the Sydney political scene. He deals with the immigrant flow, somewhat akin to a later counsellor, Professor Blainey. George protests:

The emigration to our shores is just now very great, every vessel lands a swarm, no less than 70 persons came out upon one ship ... these seemd with scarcely an exception respectable. I went on board for the purpose of examining how suitable accommodation could possibly be provided in so small a Ship and upon viewing the small comfortless holes I ...did not believe that Men would tolerate ..,such a place though ever so eager to come out here and partake of the Milk and Honey ...believe(d.) to flow without end.

He satirically writes of the false impressions of New South Wales given out by some entrepreneurs; of the dandies who

journey this far you would suppose for the sole ...purpose of showing the latest fashions and most approved Airs and Attitudes with no small share of self respect and Importance they walk and strut Upon our stage...

Ah ! The Georgian gentleman bucaneers, no doubt!

George continues his lovely tirade about British convicts: by which I am even more convinced he has no knowledge of Mary... Molly's peccadillo of 1791.

You must know some of our most immaculate Settlers have been in a very rude manner shipped off with some disagreeable appendages to the legs called Irons to the settlements of New Castle and Port Macquarie places appropriate for the reception of malefactors from this place, it is I believe a reasoned maxim that an Ass can wear a lion's skin for a season only...

He details the new restrictions on selling up grants of land for profit rather than development. Family reports deal with his brother-inlaw Mr Thomson who was not long afterwards to become an officer of the state civil service, and still later an embezzler. George's personal news is interesting- although he has condemned settlers who do not farm their grants of land, he, without any intention of farming appears to accept land himself from the Governor... Vide:

My principal business at Port Dalrymple is to take possession of Fourteen Hundred Acres of Land which Sir Thomas *(Brisbane)* has given me upon the present system of a Man to each 100 acres, I shall return to Sydney in about four months unless my Elder Brothers advise me to remain and turn Farmer but I do Do Not Know how I should... reconcile myself to such a life...

He longs to go to Europe, to be given a Commission in the Army, to gain wisdom, enjoy cultured intellectuals in a wider society, not amongst the money hungry of the Colony.

Brother James has joined Tom (2) the eldest son in a

Copartnership... at Port Dalrymple *(Launceston)*, this is indeed an inconsiderable place compared with Hobart Town and not by any means so flourishing... to carry on business at Port Dal. where they would have... little opposition as their Joint means would enable them to command the market; at this place too all their landed property Cattle and Sheep lie. They purpose blending Commerce with Agriculture... they possess upward of 300 Acres...

Oh Mother Mary Reibey, how well you tutored your sons in the ways of business! How well indeed had she herself succeeded in the previous eleven years.

Two sisters have married. Celia to Mr Thomas Wills, a son of the deceased partner of their ship building father Thomas Reibey, and Sister Eliza to the indefatigable Mr Thomson. Internal dating is provided by the recording of Sydney Gazettes, from First Nov. to the Sixth of February 1823 which are to accompany this screed to David Hope. He adds;

I would have sent according to your desire the Australian Magazine had I thought it worth your notice... nothing more to say in this letter in my next I shall touch fully upon the present Govt.... one small Commission - it is to send me out McKenzies treatise upon Phrenology.

George Reibey died on 26th October of that year, with an illness, probably consumption, following an accident when a tree fell upon him.

From George Reibey of Sydney to His cousin David Hope.

WHILE AN EXTREMELY LONG LETTER, THERE IS MUCH MEAT... HISTORICALLY SPEAKING, IN THIS LETTER. Note the great improvement in spelling, a greater use of present day standard spelling;the serious discussion upon the Macquarie-Marsden dispute,the Emancipist question... which constantly puzzles one. Did George suspect his mother's emancipist status? Where thought necessary some notes are interspersed throughout this very long account by George Reibey, at the time aged 22 years.N.I.

Australia
Sydney 14th February 1823.

Mr David Hope

Dear Cousin

I shall endeavour by the length of this Letter to pay up my arrears being at present in debt for your favours of the 28th Decem. 21 and 28th Feby 22 / accompanying the latter I received 8 Numbers of the Edin. Revue... free from the hands of Mr Browne for which receive my acknowledgements, to have them second hand as you observe will serve my purpose quite as well as at the full price / indeed much better/ though not myself of a very thrifty saving turn I can admire a judicious economy whether displayed in trifleing or momentary affairs I shall aim at following the practical example of so good a Standard,/ it pleased me to find that you believed me to be above the weak vanity which would much rather pay for the whole Feast than another should have the first taste/ with respect to the merit of the Edin. Review I agree with you, and think that it exceld every other work of the Kind in Europe which led me to make choice of it in my first letter to you however I beg it to be understood that my judgement is confined to Britain being pretty well read in most of her best Authors / France may or may not have a production of equal merit / ignorance on this head compels me to shut my mouth and of course to suppress the opinion,

I learn that France is a Nation deeply learned and far advanced in literature consequently it behoves one to be cautious in speaking upon the merits of our own Authors lest we are supposed from National prejudice to overlook or not duly appreciate the labours of any other individuals whether French,

Italian or Turk.

The character of Mr Jeffry I have been acquainted with some time, of his powerful talents I am a great admirer, and cannot say that I dislike his politicks / were you to ask me my reasons for this preference perhaps the answer would be common place and unsatisfactory; some men range themselves at once on the side of the weaker party without giving the merits of the quarrel any consideration , perhaps this is my case—and perhaps you will think me an egoist for saying so. I have observed the Wig faction possess in a much greater proportion men of real talent who by dint of ability only are enabled to keep anything like a footing against the all powerful influence of Tories and Placemen / many of these it has struck me crouch under the Arm of power from a conviction of what would be their comparative insignificance were they to join the Party among whom to be in any wise distinguished. Common sence is a great requisate/ if what I have said should clash with your ideas tell me so and I will endeavour to convince myself of my error and get rid of my present prepossession in favour of a set of men whom I have principally known through the medium of Newspapers / perhaps calculated to convey but a very limited Knowledge of their true motives and principals. I am frequently told that an examination for a short time of men and manners in England would change my sentiments upon many subjects ,/ this, I cannot believe notwithstanding Goldsmith himself tells us

> "That life is a Book of which he whose observations have been confined to his own Native Country has only read a single page"

I trust however that I should at all times be open to conversion.

Should I want Books at any time I will avail myself of your obliging offer to send them out to me but we obtain them here almost with as great facility as in England , by giving a discretional order./ you might send some that I have already, my collection now being pretty good . The works of your ingenious Countryman Sir W. Scott I have long since read,/ scarcely one of His Poems or Novels have escaped me from the Lady of the Lake to the very inferior production upon Waterloo from Waverly to the Buccaneers/ this last disappointed my expectations/ whether it or the Monastery is best I cannot determine, and perhaps it will become me better to withold an opinion, lest a remark which I have some where read should be applied to me

"That every Man especially at an age when most... of experience and apprehension of being mistaken should put him upon his guard ought to be very cautious how he passed judgement upon Writers of established merit for fear it should happen to him as it does to a great many to blame what he does not understand."

If I thought Henry Grey Bonner could turn your extract from my Letter to our advantage I would surprise him with something more of the same kind from myself, but I doubt it That same Right Honble Gent you must know has had the misfortune (tho' a Wig) to fall a little under my displeasure for his very unwarranted attack upon Genl. McQuarie our late worthy Governor than whom a more strictly upright and Moral Man will never again rule over us, nor one who will show himself more truly alive to the best interests of the Colony by his laborious assiduity for its advancement and reformation/ I am much astonished to find that the Revd. Mr Marsden has found means to create so general and so strong a feeling in his (OWN) favour throughout Britain, and at the expence of the worthy Personage abovementioned, / we here can best judge which of the two deserves it most. The great host of Religionists headed by the great Wilberforce seem to have long sought the ruin of a meritorious Man, acting unwittingly upon the most exaggerated and unfounded complaints; in the Country however the Revd. Gentn. alluded to stands alone ,his spiritual Brethren on their arrival here invariably change sentiments towards him.

The Commissioners Report I find is at last come forth, a few copies are now in the Colony, but I have not yet seen one. McQuarie as we expected is severely lashed and Marsden much excelled. / it is now almost the sole topic of the Day, nothing I believe ever excited a stronger sensation here, which is increased by the Copies being so scarce and the utter impossibility at present of getting them out of the hands of the few individuals to whom they are sent / everyone therefore is enquiring of his Neighbour if he has seen the Report or heard anything that is in it. Should this chance to be the case whatever it may be it is swallowed with the greater avidity. Should I be lucky enough to get it into my hands before the Vessel sails by which this Letter is forwarded I will let you know what will be the effect that in my opinion it is likely to produce in the event of the British Govt.adopting the Measures it may recommend though from what I can collect a total silence is observed upon the score at present/ and that everything respecting the future direction of our affairs will be treated of in a continuation, a great many individuals well known here are rather roughly handled and some deservedly, but if all I hear is true , a great portion is irrelevant abuse, foreign to the purpose of his mission ,and in no way calculated to further its ends while I admit that it was his particular province to make a faithful representation of the public Actions of public Men I think it made no part of his duty to animadvert upon the private conduct of private Men, deserve it or not, supposing however that he had the right to do so, its impolicy is obvious, / indelible disgrace is fixed upon them, which does not perish... but is handed down to their Posterity - and if in this place, the Sins of the Fathers are to be visited upon the Children every scheme for reformation will be thwarted - every laudable excursion paralysed- if an enquiry was instituted into the Character of every man in the British Dominions, very few among those whom the World designate just and honourable if 'weighted in the balance' but would be found wanting and without any real claim to such distinction, / We know that the man does not breathe who can take a retrospect of his past life with guiltless satisfaction,- Should not some attention be paid to the way in which a Person sent here has conducted himself since he committed the offence that made him for a time an outcast, if it has been exemplary will any feeling liberal minded man say he ought not be reinstated in Society?–No–to what end? / and then are these wounds so sensibly felt by him , and healed by good behaviour, again torn open, and he once more to answer as it were for crimes which by being harrowed up after the lapse of so many years places him in the same degraded point of view in which he stood as a culpret answering for them at the Bar of justice - Perhaps you will think the above stricture premature as I have not yet read the Report but those that have say that it contains a great deal of abstract matter and a very few palpably erronious statements- / if so they will not fail in appearing before the British Public in a proper shape / two of the principal personages attacked are now in England, Messrs Redfern and Eagar / men possessed of good abilities and great local Knowledge, therefore quite competent to cope with Mr Bigge.

NOTE: WM. REDFERN 1774 -1833 A QUALIFIED SURGEON OF THE BRITISH FLEET,HAVING TAKEN PART IN THE HOVE MUTINY OF THE FLEET ARRIVED IN SYDNEY 14/12/1801 AS A PRISONER.ASSISTED KING AT NORFOLK, PARDONED 1803/MACQUARIE CONFIRMED REDFERN AS A SURGEON PUTTING HIM IN CHARGE OF THE NEW HOSPITAL IN 1816. MOST SUCCESSFUL AND POPULAR... REPORTED CALAMITOUS CONDITIONS ON BOARD TRANSPORTS, AND ON PUBLIC HEALTH. 1818 LD BATHURST, SEC. OF STATE (BRIT) ORDERED BIGGE REPORT: REDFERN WAS APPOINTED BY MACQUARIE AS A MAGISTRATE WHICH WAS DIRECTLY OPPOSITE TO BIGGE ADVICE NOT TO USE EMANCIPISTS... JUDGE FIELD FOLLOWED A RULING FROM BRITAIN THAT PERSONS FREED ONLY BY THE GOVERNOR'S PARDON AND NOT BY A PARDON UNDER 'THE GREAT SEAL OF LONDON' COULD NOT MAINTAIN PERSONAL ACTION AT LAW OR ACQUIRE, RETAIN OR TRANSMIT PROPERTY. A GREAT PROTEST MEETING IN SYDNEY SENT REDFERN AND EAGAR TO LONDON TO STATE THE POINT OF VIEW OF THE COLONISTS.

ED. EAGAR 1787 -1866- IRISH LAWYER AND MERCHANT , SON OF A LANDOWNER
WAS CONDEMNED TO DEATH FOR UTTERING AND FORGING A BILL, SENTENCE
COMMUTED TO TRANSPORTATION BEYOND THE SEAS, ARRIVED IN SYDNEY BY
THE PROVIDENCE IN 1811... BECAME A TEACHER, ORGANISED BIBLE CLASSES
CONDITIONALLY PARDONED BY MACQUARIE IN 1813, BECAME A LAWYER, BUT
DENIED BY JUDGE FIELD ON THE ABOVE GROUNDS SO PRACTISED AS A
MERCHANT... ABSOLUTE PARDON IN 1818 BUT AGAIN HIS TRADING WITH KING
POMARE OF FIJI WAS QUASHED AS HE WAS AN EMANCIPIST..BECAME SEC OF
COLONISTS COMMITTEE TO ADVISE REGENT ON CIVIL AND COMMERCIAL
DISABILITIES..ARGUED FOR AN INDEPENDENT COUNCIL AND ASSEMBLY.VERY
CLOSE TO WC WENTWORTH / BY THE LATTER ALLEGEDLY EAGAR'S WIFE HAD A
CHILD IN ADDITION TO THE 4 LEGITIMATE..
    GEORGE'S LETTER CONTINUES

in fact one of the objects of their voyage was to meet that Gentn. upon his own
Ground, and reply to the aspertions they knew he was about to cast upon
them / both it is true unfortunately came Prisoners to this Country, but have
maintained an unimpeachable character (AS OF 1823) ever since their arrival
- which together with their superior talents have procured them much influence
and esteem among those who came here under the same circumstances, /
they have consequently been looked upon as the 'Leaders' of this party
between which and a certain set here, a violent enmity and jealousy exists -
these latter pride themselves upon having come out <u>free</u> but not content with
conscious superiority which this circumstance assuredly gives them- they
catch at every opportunity to evince their contempt and dislike by the most
arrogant demeanour and unfeeling expressions, the real cause is a jealousy of
the increasing importance which the superior wealth of this class of the
community is daily giving to them no hesitation is made in saying that a
<u>fellow</u> who has been a convict should not be allowed to hold property and
they would fain make it appear that in virtue of their condescension in coming
among such <u>vile refuse</u> — the distance, too, considered — all the Loaves and
Fishes should be wrested from the creatures and given as a compensation
for the honour done the place by their presence-/this feeling was carried so
far as to be broached in one of our Courts of Justice the Judge *(Field)* of
which is a person I have mentioned, /He took great pains to search for and
examine musty old statutes and succeeded in finding one which provided
that no subject once convicted of a Felony shall at any after time be allowed
to possess Property in his own right/ this has never been acted upon here ,
but was delivered with great emphasis to a crowed court as the Law of the
Land. The great proportion of the people are here for Offences do not come

within this statute- therefore the sensation excited by such a declaration was not very great, however upon being more maturely considered it was received as a dangerous point gained that might lead to something more comprehensive - the whole body of what are termed the <u>Emancipists</u> took the alarm, called a <u>general</u> Meeting and came to the resolution of appealing to the British Parliament / In pursuance of which Messrs Redfern and Eagar were deputed to lay their representations before the House of Commons, to enable them to meet every expence in doing so - they were furnished with about £1,000 Subscribed by the Meeting - though if it is true that the Commissioner himself recommends that the abovementioned Law which places the Effects of the Emancipated Felons in jeopardy should be abolished, all further proceeding on the part of Mr Eagar will be unnecessary. Should it ultimately turn out that we have formed an erroneous estimate of the value of Mr Bigg's mission to the Colony, I opine that you will set us down as a narrow-minded - prejudiced set - if you are not heavily sick, tired, and impatient of the tedious length of my treatise upon colonial politicks you will read on and hear the excuse I should make in such a case / but if on the contrary it is as uninteresting as I suspect and poor patience being worn to a skeleton, expires here the luckless Australians! what conclusions will be drawn to your disadvantage by my sober calculating headed Cousin. How is it he will say that these opinions are so widely diffused - upon what have these frail mortals at the Antipodes founded such notions and formed such gloomy anticipations when things it appears have turned out so diametrically opposite - they do not consult the Entrails of Beasts or the flight of Birds as in days of yore neither can I attribute it to the climate which is not of a nature to produce that vapourish disposition to view always the dark side of things - what is it then he will say to himself. Why nothing short of downright Rank prejudice - and I will prove it, - out of the mouth of one of their own body will I convict them, who forsooth has had the effrontery to say in one part of this letter that he has become <u>prejudiced</u> in favour of a set of men here without being able to assign any thing like a reasonable reason why - what therefore is this person's predominant passion? it does not require an answer - consequently as I believe him to be a fair specimen I conclude that they have all been activated by the same feeling in their speculations upon the results of Mr Bigg's Report and not worthy of a <u>sensible</u> Man's further notice. - But stop - it has just occured to me that I have said in one of my Letters. That I take great interest in the affairs of this Country to give them up too precipitately will not seem so and upon second thoughts. I had better first read a little more of this tiresome letter.

When I tell you that the Commissioner immediately on his arrival attached himself closely to the party I have spoken of as so hostile to the interests of the Emancipated Colonists and was evidently both in word and deed throughly infected with their illiberality you will think with me that they had great cause to apprehend the words from him. My good Cousin resumes - well this is a tolerable apology and may do, but had they been anything better than short sighted dolts without one particle of penetration they would have at once seen the refined policy of Mr B's conduct in adopting the best method of drawing out all these real sentiments by a deceiving sympthay This my dear Cousin was a motive I at one time was willing to attribute to him, it doubtless would have been wise plan had there been a sincere desire on the part of Mr Biggs to secure(?) the interests of one part of the community against the power and malignity of the others, but the nicest resolver of doubtful cases would view this in the light only of a possibility and to be rejected in favour of a conclusion drawn from 'Word and deed.' Notwithstanding however all that has been said and done, the words of the people are satisfied that whatever may be the ulterior purposes of God(?) with regard to New South Wales it will continue to preserve its character for justice and moderation, should we unfortunately be mistaken, other sentiments than those of loyalty and attatchment to the Mother Country will develope themselves as time advances; the Native born's of even the first generation are not so void of reflection or common sence as not to value themselves upon personal freedom and equal system of laws: before I conclude this subject I cannot refrain from once more recommending the character of the Govr. Macquarie to your notice. I am anxious to impress upon your mind a thorough persuasion of his worth - it would give me much pleasure if my humble efforts should be any wise instrumental in doing ,justice to a man whose most heartfelt pleasure during his arduous administration here was to promote the welfare of such as manifested a return of virtuous(?) feelings and good conduct what can be a nobler undertaking than to(?) snatch a poor lost fellow creature from the vortex of Sin and misery — to restore a useful agent to society by those well directed means which had Govr. McQuarie been weak or vile enough to give up in favour of the opinions of the Set here who are shameless enough enough to contend that for Convicts this is a place of <u>punishment</u> exclusively, and that for example sake no other consideration should influence the conduct of the Govt towards them, had this injudiceous system I say been pursued, those that now form the most important and valuable part of the population of New South Wales would have been languishing in Slavery and wretchedness, not the protectors but the disturbers of Society: does he then whose disinterested benevolence has made so many of his fellow-men happy desire to be thought and spoken of with horror (as is the case in Scotland) as the determined opponent of all good works- the merciless persecutor of that paragon of holiness Saint Samuel, were the good people of your Country, those I mean who deem themselves specially called upon to execrate the name of the tyrant, and foe of religion, but whose zeal I am afraid hurry them to judgement upon ex-parte evidence were they coolly to examine should an opportunity offer, the portly carcase - round fat jolly red face and laughing eyes of the said Saint of ours whom I have no doubt they have been accustomed to view in imagination as the very type of mortification and woe with the pale emaciated visage thin spare form and dozen sorrowful etceteras, the usual consequence of deep care, me thinks it would strike them that the appearance of the Man indicated very little suffering either in mind or body, which together with the testimony of every old inhabitant in the place ought to be proof sufficient to refute the unfavourable opinions entertained of Genl. Macquarie respecting his conduct to Mr Marsden - you may judge for yourself of the degree of estimation this worthy man is held in when I tell you that on his ensuing Birthday there are to be no less than four Public Dinners in the single Town of Sydney - If Mr Wilberforce was aware that instead of those mighty things atchieved among the Savages of New Zealand by Mr Marsden there is comparatively nothing done for the advancement of Religion and civilisation, and that through mismanagement and the bad Conduct of the Missionaries the Natives have taken a disgust at the former which many years will not efface / his present opinion of Mr M might be a little staggered / you will scarcely credit what profligacy that some of these Ministers have attained, it is a fact that one of them keeps several of the Native Women under the very eyes of his Wife. Some credit would have been due to Mr Marsden if he had turned his attention in the spiritual way to our own Aboriginees but it unluckily happens that these poor wretches have neither Pork nor Flax to give for the saving of their Souls; when our native institution was suggested by Govr.Macquarie Mr Marsden could not be prevailed upon to give his assistance or countenance to it upon what principle I could never learn, but it is thought that he was chagrined that any but himself should have been the first promoter or that his opinion of their intellects was so contempable that he despaired of ever being able to bring them to the Knowledge of a God, the result has provd(?) that such a surmise would-have been fallacious for under proper treatment these truly benighted race have manifested a degree of intelligence which I thought was not in their nature, they are notwithstanding the lowest species of human beings, and consequently it is an arduous task to undertake to draw such from a state of barbarism and adapt them to the purposes of Society - That they have degenerated from a state of nature is clear from a comparison with other newly discovered people by the most wimsical casuist it cannot be contended that nature who has bestowed such various faculties on man should originally have designed these for so abject a condition, Inured to privation of almost every kind they find in ease apparently their only comfort, From habitual indolence they have become supine and slothful, their ideas extending no further than the objects within their view, and from thence it follows that their language must be very confined as it can embrace little more than the names of places and the Animal and Vegetable productions of the climate, In their infancy they must be treated tenderly, in order that as they grow up they may look back with aversion to their primitive condition and feel the more sensibly their obligation to providence and to us as its immediate instruments in releasing them from a state of misery and want. They should feel as we do that to the continuance of the comforts they enjoy something must be necessary, as nothing can be obtained without an endeavour to procure it. These endeavours closely connected constitute a life of industry to the measure of which a short experience would acquaint them those enjoyments would be proportioned and industry arising from necessity would be as acceptable to them as to any of the people.

The emigration to our shores is just now very great, every vessel lands a swarm, no less than seventy (70) persons came out upon one Ship a short time since / as these seemed with scarcely an exception respectable I went on board for the purpose of examining how suitable accomodations could possibly be provided for so many in so small a Ship and upon viewing the small comfortless holes I then met with did not before believe that Men would tolerate an existance in such a place though ever so eager to come out here and partake of the Milk and Honey which the sanguine minds of many together with the high coloured representation of Mr Jeffrys and others leads them to beleive flows without end / Ours is undoubtedly a fine Country, both as to Soil and Climate, but nothing extraordinary nor worthy of the extravagant praise that has been bestowed upon it by such enthusiasts as Mr J, the best guide for a Settler to go by that I have yet seen (excepting the valuable Worth(?)) of my Countryman Wentworth(?) is a small publication written by a Captain Dixon the commander of a ship called the Skelton that was out here about 2 years ago / it has no pretensions to literary worth, but is a simple and unvarnished relation of facts / it represents as far as the truth will warrant the advantages resulting from Emigration to N.S.W. without concealing ny of the difficulties that present themselves to the surprise and disappointment of most Settlers, several have returned in disgust but these I am happy to say are such as we shall never have to regret the losing of — indeed we have had many character imported of late years whose absence could have been borne without any serious injury to the interests of the Country, who like sickly stagnant waters taint the atmosphere without fertilizing the Soil / They journey this far you would suppose for the sole and generous purpose of showing the latest fashions and most approved Airs and attitudes, with no small share of self respect and importance they walk and strut a very little more than an hour upon our stage before they are hurled back to their native insignificance, a short experience shows that something more than a well made coat and imposing manner is necessary to persuade us they are genuine Gentlemen; a disappointment in this respect frequently operates in depriving our Society of those honourable members, / and by the bye in several instances lately in such a way as left no choice to the parties for you must know some of our most immaculate Settlers have been in a very <u>rude</u> <u>manner</u> shipped off with some disaggreable appendages to the legs called Irons to the Settlements of New Castle and Port Macquarie places appropriated for the recept on of Malefactors from this place, it is I believe a reasoned maxim that an Ass can wear a Lion's skin for a season only, the moral is applicable to these Gentlemen, there is something that we call behaviour that is amediately and uniformly understood The plainest peasant or labourer will say of a man whom he esteems in a certain way, He is a Gentleman every bit of him, and he is perfectly understood by all who hear him not rank in life but a turn of mind a tenor of conduct that is amiable and worthy and the ground of confidence. Formerly it was very common for Settlers to remain here only a sufficient length of time to get their land measured - to take up the Grant - and then to steal away having first taken care to pocket a little cash the proceeds of the Farm which was amediately Sold to one of the Residents / this very fraudulent practice has been effectivally remedied by some late Order regulating the distribution of Land, and which will have the judicious tendency of proportioning the Grant to the Capital / heretofore recommendatory letters to Men in power have in a very many instances been suffered to have an undue influence, that a poor Emigrant possessed of these have succeeded in obtaining larger Grants than the real Capitalist(?) who had the means of carrying into effect every thing required of him by the Govt. and added a real benefit to the Colony by the introduction of his property, the present system requires the Emigrant for every Hundred Acres located to him to support a Man from his own means permanently. consequently for 1,000 Acres he must take ten men? I hear such an incumbrance as this will require no mean Capital which consideration will induce every one who is not imprudent enough to risk the loss of his all to take no more than upon a calculation he will find he can safely support, some have indeed laid the foundation of their inevitable ruin by departure from this line of conduct among whom is your <u>friend</u> Browne, if he really is such by the way I must in confidence tell you I never could suffer this Gent. to bear the same relation to me not that I know any thing of him inconsistant with the character of an honest man, but there is something so disgustingly obtrusive and unrefined in his nature with which the longer is your acquaintance the less you feel disposed to that 'Sweet communion of Souls' which characterizes true friendship and esteem; if he did not quarrel with every Passenger coming out his manner and disposition bred such a dislike of him, that all with scarcely an exception keep him at the greatest distance / if Mr Miller came by the same Vessel I think a very worthy young man Mr Thomson and he are distantly related from standing in the same degree of affinity to a Mr Young who gave them both Letters to Sir Thomas Brisbane, but I am sorry to say very little notice has been taken of either one o the others. Mr T indeed from having a little personal Knowledge of his Excely. recd. the most attention but these consisted in empty professions and unperformed promises / the truth is that his Philosophical speculations ocupy so much time that little can be spared for friend or the duties of his Govt. which I am grieved to say are most shamefully neglected, instead of the affairs of the Colony being in that flourishing and rapidly improving state which characterized the active administration of Govr. Macquarie / they have been cramped and almost ruined by a series of injurious measures, a want of energy and a total disregard for the interests of the Country in the present Rulers, This is a sweeping charge you will say but I assure you it is not the less true / I have written so much this time otherwise would enter more into particulars upon this subject, however will not fail to do so some time or other suffice it to say that Sir Thomas either from supineness of reluctance to abstract himself in the least from more momentous affairs (?) upper regions has thrown ours entirely into the hands of Mr Gouldbourn the Colonial Secty. (a mere understrapper from Downing Street) a person who has neither ability or inclination to do us good. Mr Thomson is now at Port Dalrymple V.D.L. waiting patiently for the appointment of Naval Officer to that place which I believe is to take place shortly, upwards of 12 Months have elapsed since he had the first promise of it from Sir Thomas who led him to expect that immediately on his arrival at Port Da. the Situation would be given to him in consequence of which Mr T. set off for that place forthwith where to his great surprise and disappointment he learnt from Leiut. Govr. Sorrell that the appointment was about to be confirmed to Leiut. Kenworthy who was then doing the duty, this person held another situation at the same time equally as good which is inconsistant with our Colonial laws when vested in the same person permanently, the propriety of a division therefore suggested itself and Mr T. was in hope either one or the other would be given to him by an order from head quarters as soon as an explanation had taken place with Sir Thomas / but he was disappointed, and after a vexatious and expensive delay of several months returned in despair to this place accompanyed by Mrs T. and infant Daughter. Our Mother who was then on a visit to the part of the family(?) residing at Port Dalrymple - advised him to this step and came back the same time. As soon as Captain Wood who lives on the Hobart Town side of the Country heard of the departure of Mr T. he waited upon Leiut. Govr. Sorrell and expostulated with him upon the treat ment Mr T. had recd. / the Govr. then told him that if Mr Thomson would return he would in a short time arrange it for Mr T. to have the Naval Officership and Kenworthy the other for a permancency instead - Captn. Wood amediately wrote to Mr T. strongly advising him to try his luck once more in Van Diemens, he has done so, however before his departure he had an interview with the Govr. in Chief who furnished him with another letter to Sorrell desiring that he might have the appointment, which by the next arrival we are in hopes to hear has taken place. In about three Weeks I myself leave this *(Sydney)* for Port Dalrymple having under my protection Mrs Thomson who was left here with us until Mr T. was certain he was not again deceived / indeed it behoves one to provide well against the bad faith of the present Govr. Sir Thomas had power without doing injustice to any one to appoint Mr Thomson at once and have saved the delay and anxiety which he occasioned him by his undecisive letters which were couched in such a style as to leave it almost optional with Sorrell whether he noticed them or not.

My principal business at Port Da1rimple is to take possession of Fourteen Hundred Acres of Land which Sir Thomas has given me upon the present system of a Man to each 100 acres, I shall return to Sydney in about four Months unless my Elder Brothers advise me to remain and turn Farmer, but I do not Know how I should at present be able to reconcile myself to such a life, my desire is first to make a voyage to Europe and see something of the World, but to accomplish this requires better friends than my own individual Self is in possession of / and to go solely depending upon our good Mother is an incumbrance I never could think of loading her with. Oftentimes I have wished that His Majesty had me for one of his Military Servants and a more Zealous and loyal one perhaps he may not have though a far distant Australation(?), how unlucky it is that the said illustrious personage is not fully aware of the great acquisition I should be to his interests, Why in imagination alone I have in the field atchieved the most wondrous deeds, if therefore they wish them done in reallity give me but a Commission and an oppertunity and then —— If it was my fortune to possess a friend in some very great Man (as for instance Dr Chalmers) I should apply to him forthwith to use his interest in obtaining for me what at present is my greatest ambition a Commission in the Army Stationed though almost any where but here, this you know would be my passport in all climes as a Gent and would put me in possession of the means tho (?) at first moderate of obtaining Wisdom I mean that since Knowledge of the World which I have laboured hard to gain through the medium of Books, in this Country the means of enlarging the mind by observation and intercourse with your fellows is very confined especially as jealosies and party feeling runs so high moreover the great bulk of our Society is composed of Adventurers and others whose main object is the bettering of their condition. The conversation therefore seldom runs upon any topic save what may amediately concern the speaker and such as no one whose mind is bent upon any thing but money making would feel any interest in.

My Brother James has entered into Copartnership with our elder Brother Thomas and gone to reside at Port Dalrymple, this is indeed rather an inconsiderable place compared with Hobart Town and not by any means so flourishing, but the competion had of late become so great at the latter settlement, in consequence of the amazing influx of Settlers, as to produce a very sensible effect upon the profits of James' business, and as an improvement was not likely to take place, Thomas and he wisely agreed to unite their Capital and carry on business at Port Dal. where they comparatively would have little opposition as their joint means would enable them to command the Market; at this place too all their landed property Cattle and Sheep lie. They purpose blending Commerce with Agriculture, the latter to be conducted by Thomas and the former by James, thrive they must, both are too prudent to enter into any wild Speculation, neither is encumbered with debt, and their property in land and Stock is now very considerable / of the former they possess upward of 3,000 Acres without the burden which as I have before stated is urged by the present system, of Horned Cattle they have nearly 500 Head and of Sheep about 2,000 - all of which is exclusive of their Stock in Trade, House, &c -

Of the Marriage of our Sister Eliza I need not speak, by the bye if we guessed right you were desirous that a great part of the World should be made acquainted with such an occurance as we have seen it in many of the Scotch and English papers which we concluded got in through no other channel than yours, if this is the case you will observe that you made a mistake in saying that Mr Thomson came out as one of the Suit of Sir Thomas Brisbane.

Eliza and Elizabeth, daughters of Mary Reibey
Photographs courtesy of Pat Pickering, ACT

1807– 1854
Mrs. Jane Penelope Atkinson née Reibey
Miniature portrait, watercolour on ivory
State Library of New South Wales

Before you are no doubt made acquainted with the Marriage of our Sister Celia to Mr Thomas Wills of whom I believe you had previously heard a little, such an event was to me a gratifying circumstance as from our infancy him and I have been on terms of the strictest intimacy and friendship / our tempers and dispositions are heretofore well known to each other, and I will venture to say very few in the World possess characters more amiable and honourable than his in every respect, add to this a handsome person and gentlemany manners, but these you will say are secondary considerations, true with the moralist, but not the ladies, and I have my suspicions that they had no small weight with my good Sister long before She visited your Shores, You see, I have pestered you a good deal with our family affairs but your very kind attention to our Mother and Sisters, the very high terms in which they at all times speak of you, as well as your evident interest in our family matters we regard you as a member of it more nearly allied to us than our real tie of consanguinity warrants / henceforth I shall consider you as a <u>Brother</u> and as a consequent to this title endowed with all the privileges thereto appertaining which I take to consist in the right of giving wholesome advice and admonition intermixed when necessary with a proper share of censure - an unreserved developement of opinions and sentiments, which I trust will at all times be mutual.

By the Minerva I send you Sydney Gazettes from the First Nov. to the Sixth of February 23 also an allmanack for the present year, I would have sent according to you desire the Australian Magazine had I thought it worth your notice. according to your request I addressed the Parcel cont. the Newspapers and Almanack to the care of Charles Corran, & Co. Leith

I have written to your Brother Mr John Hope but have not yet received any answer, If I was sure Wm. could spare the time taken up in answering a letter (but which I conclude his Elder Br. had not at disposal) I would drop him a few lines upon the state of Religion here.

I believe I have nothing more to say in this letter in my next I shall touch fully upon the present Govt.

> In conclusion I have Dear Sir to
> assure you of the affection &
> esteem of
> Geo. Reibey

N.B.

I will trouble you with one small Commission - it is to send me out McKenzies treatise upon "Phrenology."

Letter 8

To Cousin David Hope, Glasgow.

From the second brother James Haydock Reibey. 17/9/1823. Launceston, Port Dalrymple, Van Deimans (sic) Land.

This is the letter of a much more mature young man. James is 3 years senior to his learned young brother George. Moreover he is married; and within the past year has made the big move to the North to take up a 'copartnership' with his elder brother Thomas. Like his brother George, James didn't fancy Launceston…but since his business was failing, he joined his generous older brother in this splendid copartnership…

Interesting freighting by brig and travelling by Gig over the 127 miles between the two centres in the early 19th century. As visitors now know, that route by its very nature was the busy highway ,the joining access. It is rich in Tasmanian history.

The Reibey brothers by now were well established,between them mustering 400 head of cattle, 2000 sheep,various farms , Stores and premises in town (Launceston).

This memo of course clearly dates the National Treasure, Entally.

> My brother *(Thomas)* is building a beautiful house on his Estate called Entally, which has now cost him about Six Hundred Pounds.

The pragmatic James tell all the family news. Most interesting is the short acount of his disagreement with his mother, Mary Reibey concerning his marriage to Rebecca. So Mary could be tough with her children!

> …you *(that is David Hope)*, will Rather wonder probably how I have got on so well without any assistance from My Mother, for you are probably aware that my Mother discarded me after my marriage, there was just reasons for her doing so then I was only seventeen years of age and my wife unknown to her Tho She *(Mary Reibey)* has often said since I have made a wise choice , in fact , I have for it is now nearly Eight years since we where first marriage we have lived as happy as possible & she has been a good helpmate to me…

He reports that his Mother is well & hearty in Sydney, Thomas & his Lady live happily with their three children 8 miles off in the country (Entally)

His next news covers the sad illness of George , the youngest brother; it proved to be a fatal illness, probably consumption agravated by the tree accident. .

as exercise was recommended to him , (he) used to amuse himself with cutting trees down... one fell on him, he lay about 100 yards from the house for above an hour, nobody having seen him, he at last crawled into, the house.

The graphic tale of the flooded creek, the distance and delay of medical help is vividly reported by James.

Poor George the Pride and Flower of the flock to be snatched away at 21 years...

But the family tragedy is doubled with a similar terminal illness of sister Celia after the birth of her child.

It appears that both were smitten by the scourge of the 19th century, consumption (tuberculosis).Sister Ellza and husband Lieut. Thomson also live in Launceston, he a Naval Officer... John Atkinson, son of the old man who cared for Mary and her two girls in London in 1820-21 has offered marriage to Jane Penelope she is only fifteen, Handsome and more clever than the two Eldest .

I know she has a most excellent genius and very apt. she is much larger than the others but stout in proportion.

James makes very plain the agricultural situation in these lovely Eastern river flats of V.D.L.;

at near distances to the Town it is pretty well occupied , there has a vast accession arrived lately of settlers, particularly Scotch the whole with a very few exceptions have Settled in Van Diemans Land ... the General Grants of land given to the Emigrants is from 500 to 2000 Acres according to the Amount of the Capital they invest in the Colony... if you bring out good Letters to the Governor or the Lieut, Governor.

James wished David Hope to hire a Scot to migrate out to Launceston to undertake the management of a flock of sheep to:

Improve the wool etc... I would give him £40 or £50 pr. annum...
you can engage him a Steerage passage in one of the Company's
ships ... engage him for at least five years by a written agreement
& bind him tight.

*James was about 12 years when his seafaring father died, so one must suppose that
most of this business acumen , exhibited by the young man of 25 summers, came from
his mother's training.*
This is a good letter.

To David Hope
60 Brunswick Street
Glasgow

Received Glasgow 3/1824

Launceston, Port Dalrymple
Van Deimans Land Septr. l7th 1823

My Dear Cousin,

I Received your various favours as likewise the Newspapers you was so kind
to send which in the distant part cf the Globe is always a thankful treat, Mr
Macarthur the Scotch Clergyman kept your Letters for 4 or 5 months at Hobart
Town after his arrival, nor did he send them over even after I got our agents
to apply to him for Letters for me & Mr Thomson, Mr Moodie the Commissary
at last enclosed them to me in a frank.

You will wonder to find my Letter dated in this place, but I have now to
inform you I have been there 9 months, having joined my Brother Thomas in
Copartnership in Cattle Sheep and trade generally I found by staying at Hobart
town I was losing considerably. I found it best to come & join Thomas who
had been soliciting me to do so for some years but owing to my dislike to
Launceston I was a long time in making up my mind to, one thing while at
Hobart it was a plan of mine tho probably foolish not to Run in debt having
never purchased without Cash in hand, However this Rule was beneficial in
my leaving Hobart for I was able to leave in a very short notice packed up my
Stock in trade as it was in the Stores, frieghted a Brig put that & all my furniture
on board, & came across the Country 127 Miles in a Gig.

Our Cattle here jointly consists of about four hundred Head, about two thirds my Brothers, about two Thousand Sheep, joint equal shares, besides various farms, which are principally my Brothers, Stores & premises in town which the Government offered two thousand Pounds for but my Brother (this was just before I came over) asked four thousand - our Stock in trade amt. about 3,000 Pounds I have made considerable Improvements, outhouses which by contract cost us three Hundred Pounds, this is joint Property equal Shares / My House at Hobart Town which I threw into the concern rents for One Hundred & Thirty Pounds pr. Annum, Eight Horses &c, besides these my Brother is building a beautiful House on his Estate called Entally, which has now cost him about Six Hundred Pounds. you will Rather wonder probably how I have got on so well without any assistance from my Mother, for you are probably aware that my Mother discarded me after my marriage, there was just reasons for her doing so then I was only Seventeen years of age and my wife unknown to her. Tho She has often said since I have made a wise choice, in fact I have, for it is now nearly Eight years since we where first marriage we have lived as Happy as possible & she has been a good helpmate to me, I often think now how saving I was then and how sedate we began a little Shop, with a Stock of £40 which I obtained Credit for in Sydney, and by Return the same vessell I came down in I Remitted the amount. my Wife who was Widow then 21 & was a Widow four year had a House tho in a very unfurnished state & built of Wood we managed to get two Small rooms Habitable & every Shilling that was taken was preserved with a great deal more care than I now do fifty Pounds. My mother found from various reports I was steady and doing well she forgave me, & we have been good friends ever since, but she thought I did not want any assistance, in fact I was as well without it probably, but when she was in England she wrote me word to take possession of Half the Sheep at this place, about 400. Then you see my dear cousin I am not treating you as a stranger, I have endeavoured to think while writing this Letter that you stood as a Brother rather than as a Cousin as you wish to be called in various Letters I have seen to my Sisters. I have given you a History of our property as well as I am able and hope it will be acceptable to you -

I will no give you some account of the family. Rank first my mother she is well and hearty in Sydney I heard from her a few days ago, Thomas & his Lady are quite well they live in the Country about Eight Miles off. he has now three children, a Boy he had about 4 weeks ago, named after me. then comes me and my wife, who are thank God quite well, & now my dear Cousin comes some very sorrowful news, namely my Brother George is so very Ill I am very much afraid he will not Recover, the Doctor says he does not think he will. he came down here about 4 or 5 months ago for the good of his Health, he was ordered into the Country by his Physician / he was rapidly Recovering & as exercise was recommended to him, used to amuse himself with cutting trees down, at last, one fell on him, which nearly killed him, he lay about 100 yards from the House for above an hour, nobody having seen him, he at last crawled into the house, my Brother Thomas Immediately dispatched a man on Horseback to town for Medical assistance, but unfortunately the River which is in front of his House was very high over the Banks not fordable, and the Canoe he was used to cross in was washed away the day before / the man had to ride about Ten Miles up the River to a Canoe and being very dark when he got there the people where afraid to cross him that night / he had to wait untill morn & then could not cross his horse he had to walk to town then 15 miles thro mud up to his knees all the way (you cannot conceive the state of the Roads here in Winter times / no made roads every Valley a River,- he got in about 12 OClock, with a note to me. This was about 22 hours after the accident happened, altho only 8 miles as direct Road, & to complete the Misfortune the Doctor was in the Country in another Direction attending another patient, however he came in in about half an hour after, and we immediately set off and tho we had to swim our horses 2 or 3 times in places that now are quite dry / we got out to the River in an hour, and fortunately my Brother had just before found a Smaller Canoe which we passed over one by one at the Imminent danger of our Lives, my Brothers House is just on the opposite Bank. The Doctor who is very clever (Priest) took from him 50 ounces of Blood that Evening and stopped two days with him, and used to go out every day the Roads began to mend daily & my Brother had found his big Canoe so he used to go with more facility, he was recovering fast from that calamity but has had a Relapse and we are now very much alarmed for his life, he is now in the country very Ill, too much so that he could not write to his Mother. Poor George the Pride and flower of the flock, to be snatched away at 21 years of age, in the prime of life, it is heartbreaking to think of it, and what adds more to the misery of the family is that my oldest Sister. (Celia) is from what I can learn in a similar state her complaint is I think something like George's, after giving Birth to a Daughter (who is named Alice) she was not able to suckle and has been very Ill since, my sister Jane writes it is a Consumption. I have been writing my Mother to advise her to bring Celia down here & then she can nurse George (altho he is well nursed now), Mrs Thomson & her husband is living a stones throw from us here in Launceston, he is <u>Naval officer</u> here the most respectable in the place next to the

Commandants / his Income now not above Three Hundred (£300) a year but will Increase, he was a good deal hurt about your putting in his marriage in the Gazette, as many copies came out here & as he was not on the staff of the Governor nor then in any situation whatever, it certainly made him look foolish it appeared that he had written home so / my other two Sisters are quite well. John Atkinson, a Son of Old Atkinson of London (you know him, I believe)has offered Jane marriage some time, he is a worthy young man & well off but she is too young to think of marriage, just turned fifteen. I have not seen her since my Mother took her to Sydney but they tell me she is Handsomer and more clever than the two Eldest I know she has a most excellent genius and very apt. she is much larger than the others but stout in proportion. He wrote us about it from Sydney desiring our consent & good wishes, our answer was he had our good wishes but must wait a little longer he is rather sickly which is the only objection against him.

In the morning I am going out to my Brother Thomas's to take out all the Medical advice in the place which consists of three Gentlemen all very good, one a Scotchman named Cameron came out first voyage in the Skelton but he is not so Clever as the others, and is rather brutish in his manners. Poor George I am very much alarmed for him, but as I shall not yet close this Letter I will acquaint you how he gets on & the Result of the Medical Survey.

I am very happy to find you are appointed agents in Glasgow to this New shipping company, their Capital is too Large & I am afraid it will not answer very well at all Events, I would strongly advise a ship to be sent to this Port Direct occasionally / it must not be too Large or Else she will not be able to come all the way up the river but a North Country Built Ship which generally are a light Draught of Water about 250 or 300 tons Burden would answer Better than a large one most all the Letters now come here at a very heavy expence of transporting their Goods a Second time the Freight from Hobart to here is £3.10 p/ton and very seldom you can get a chance of a vessell coming round others again Cart some of their things across at double or treble the Expence of the freightage, At all events I should strongly advise a ship coming here every Six months at present Otherwise by & by / the place is Improving wonderfully there has never been a Direct arrival from England here but one about 4 months ago / a Cutter Eighty Tons (she is now lying at my Door) with a Mr Lawrence on board her owner an adventurer or rather an Emigrant to these parts, a Ship of 1,OOO Tons has laid at Geo Town about 4 Miles inside the Heads / at present Geo Town is the,Head Quarters but it is to be abandoned & Head Quarters is coming up here again / this is a Large Town, but there is no buildings at Geo Town but.Government, only one free man in the place except the Officers, Col Cameron of the Buff; is now Commandant here he is only just come but a very good man what I see of him,

George was telling me he had written you a very long Letter about thirty pages. Thomas has promised to write to you, but he is a strange a fellow he cannot bear to write or look over accounts / he has got in Disgrace with all his friends for not writing his wishes for your Health & happiness are the same as ours, Septr. 28th

I have been out spending a week with George. I took out the Medical Men on Monday last they have held a Survey & Consultation. they agree as to the method his Physician has been using towards him to be correct / they give unfavourable hopes, but advise a Sea Voyage which he will undertake as soon as Possible to Sydney

I have enclosed you one Gazette with Mr Thomsons appointment in, but I have written to a friend of mine at Hobart Town to Enclose you Copies of an attack made by the Agricultural Society in Sydney against Van Diemans Land & the two Replies, one of them written in Sydney, the Illiberality of the Attack made by Mr Justice Field is so well known in the Colony that it has brought down Contempt on its author.

I am a sad one at writing a Letter I just put down my thoughts as they flow, & never can bear to look over a Letter after having written it in order to Correct, as I know very well it will not please me so I ever let it take its fate.

The Land this side van Diemans Land is far better than on the other both for grazing & agricultural purposes, fine plains not a tree standing on them, nothy to do but put the Plough in / but at near distances to the Towns it is pretty well occupied, there has a vast accession, arrived lately of Settlers particularly Scotch the whole with a very few exceptions have Settled in Van Diemans Land particularly along the Banks of the Macquarie River, a Space occupying about Fifty Miles that twelve Months ago was not a Hut on it is now nearly all occupied by the New Emigrants Having Settled along its banks. the General Grants of Land given to the Emigrants is from five Hundred to Two Thousand Acres according to the Amount of the Capital they Invest in the Colony, a person bringing out Three Thousand Pounds is Entitled to a Grant of Two Thousand acres or much less if you bring out good Letters to the Governor or Lt. Governor & stand high in Character or in his good opinion

Do you think you could engage a Good Man, about you that can undertake the Management of a flock of Sheep to Improve the wool &c. If you could do so for me I would give him £40 or £50 pr. Annum or I will leave it to you to make the best arrangement you can for me / you can engage him a Steerage passage in one of the Company's Ships and Draw on me for the Amt. which shall be immediately honoured you must engage him for at least five years by a Written agreement & bind him tight

I think I have said all I have to say & will now conclude this Letter by assuring you of my unalterable Esteem and sincere gratitude for your Brotherly Kindness to my Mother & Sisters in Scotland. & Remain

My Dear Cousin
Yours Sincerely
James H. Reibey

PS. Mr P. Broadfoot I have not seen by reason of my being here when he arrived, but your Letter came over safe

Our agents at Hobart Town are Messrs. Welsh & Heylin

Letter 9

From Mary Reibey to her cousin David Hope, Glasgow.

From Sydney. Feby.9th-1825.
Here is a letter written by Mary Reibey some four years after returning from her visit to Britain. She is living in George Street Sydney.

Two of her children are dead, Celia and George. She is here, in this correspondence, making business arrangements with Cousin David Hope of Glasgow. Her trading and bartering at this time was evidently still busily pursued. Otherwise there is little of Family interest. It is proof of the widow's determined merchandising . Her son Thomas and his wife Richarda together with their little daughter and two sons are well settled at Entally . Son James co- farms with Thomas at Launceston and Hadspen. Entally farming and Reibey trading goes ahead despite dangerous bushrangers according to reports . This letter is remarkable for its brevity compared with other missives.

9.2.1825
per ship Mangles
Ship Letter Plymouth
Feby 9th - 1825

My dear Cousin
by the Ship Mangles and by the Son of your Agent Mr Broadfoot of Leith I send you a few lines to say that with mysef my family here are all well health and much the same as when I last wrote you / they all desire their love and respects and are anxiously waiting letters from you / it is now sometime Since and I think it long in not receiving one from you / Mr Broadfoot has been living a short time with us and says he will see you therefore he will be able to give you more information than I Can Communicate through Paper / I think him a very amiable young man and very steady I have a very high opinion of him, I regret much not having the Money for What goods are Sold handed over to me according to Promise by this Conveyance / I should have Considered it very Safe by Mr Broadfoot but so it is I have been disapointed very much which has grieved me Sorely / I expect by the next vessel Sails from here in about a month I shall be able to send some part or all for what is sold / I should like if Possible you to apoint an Agent to receive the Money here the Agent for the Australian Company Wld. oblige you to remit the Cash with his/ I have Sent from the residue of the goods to my House from the Commission Wharehouse and Which I will endevour to sell myself they have offered 2d a lb for the paint but which I shall not take / I have inclosed for your inspection the Acct Sales, if you have not laid the Money out namely the £60 Sterling which I wrote you to do for me in goods you may Keep that with the interest and put to my Credit / having lately made use of some of your goods on my own account Which you shall have a regular Acct of whenever it will be my fortune to receive the Cash for What is actually sold;I shall not lose a moment in remitting it / I have sent by Mr Broadfoot our last years Almanack and last Sydney Gazzette with one No 17 newpaper the Australian, and the Pelin(?) for Mary, my daughter Elizabeth says she whould wish to Send you a small memorial but will defer it till another opportunity/I must Conclude this before I intended has the person has Called for them and Cannot wait / I now remain your ever affectionate friend and Cousin

    M.Reibey

Letter 10

PROBABLY THE MOST ATTRACTIVE AND DELIGHTFUL LETTER IN THIS COLLECTION. Jane Penelope Reibey has become Jane Penelope Atkinson, happily living in Sydney with husband John, while their house on the Hawkesbury-Nepean is being completed, "about 34 miles from the metropolis." Internal evidence shows that David Hope, sight unseen , has made an offer of marriage to this spirited young cousin after no doubt reading James' account and some reciprocal correspondence. Her storybook reply of an early marriage to a much loved fiancé prior to receipt of the Scot's letter of proposal is beautifully written, a sensitive letter. The letter of course deals with the death of her siblings, Celia and George and the later death of Celia's babe, Alice Wills. Then like the good methodist (I think) she is she continues in a pragmatic tone to answer his (David Hope's) questions about the Colony.

And so we learn about such amusements as

the Wanton and corrupting airs of the opera). However there is lots of noise from 'intoxicated People and the disgusting language of the Aborigine.

Maybe Mr and Mrs Atkinson are particularly restrained in their entertainments. For, looking back at Mother Mary's notes when visiting London some 5 years earlier, she and the two elder sisters, Celia and Eliza had enjoyed theatre in London, Glasgow and Edinburgh.

AS for balls.. well read her letter..both Jane's and Mary's remarks. Then there is the delightful vignette of their Boating picnics... Her mother Mary Reibey accompanying them. They gather oysters off the rocks... they take a little Bread and Butter, and a cold Dinner for an all day harbour jaunt. A delightful Breath of the 1825 Sydney residents' joys...

Sydney 9th Feby. 1825

Wednesday

I was much delighted My Dear Cousin at the receipt of your favour by the Portland which came rather unexpectedly as I had begun to fear you had not received my Letter by Minerva which was dated 7th Feby. 1823 and I did not believe your answer to be the middle of Decbr. 1824 but I suppose I must impute to the negligence and retention of Captain Bell-

You say you have often heard of me by the "Hearing of the Ear" but I am afraid my Dr. Cousin it will be a long time ere you see me by the "Seeing of the Eye" unless you take a ship to New Holland as my Husband (Mr Atkinson) has not the slightest wish either to visit England or Scotland for many years he shortly intends leasing off all his (?) and ? speculations and Commission (?) and returning to a small estate in the country about 34 Miles from the Metropolis which we are now building on and improving therefore I think there is not much hope of our ever visiting Caledonias long Famed Lakes & Valleys nothing I can assure you would give me greater pleasure were we enabled to do it —

You will see by the above that I do not now write under the name of Reibey. The advice contained in your letter was most thankfully perused as it convinced me you took some interest in my happiness but & Alas!!! it came too late indeed you must not be offended when I say that if it came before hand my heart was gone too far to return / it was irrevocably lost but do not think I was too precipitate no it was a matter of longer consideration than you would imagine / you little thought my Hand and Heart were engaged long before you received my last Letter - I own I was married rather younger than the generality of my sex but in this Country they marry so much younger than in yours / my dear Friend it was not the whim of a moment but the result of a long meditated and mature deliberation / I made it the subject of Prayer and Meditation by night as well as by day and my Heart told me that I most sincerely loved and that our love was resciprocal / indeed I think there are not many who considered the marriage state as seriously as I did - I am far from opinion that our Happiest Days are spent in virginity or courtship but on the contrary I think where two Beings are united who have one heart one mind, one soul, the maried state is much more loveable. 12 oclock P.M. I find I am getting so sleepy and writing so dreadfully bad that I must bid you good night and resume my Letter tomorrow morning —

Thursday Afternoon

3 Oclock -

You say you tremble for what our letters may (?) but you of course have heard of our most dreadful breavements long eer this / Indeed my Dr. Prince I think trouble never was like ours The loss of two such invaluable and beloved relations was enough to wring our very souls but it was the will of the Lord - yes - "for affliction cometh not of the Dust neither doth trouble spring out of the Ground" "the Lord gave and the Lord taketh away Blessed be the name of the Lord" Therefore we I trust submitted to the divine will with all the fortitude and resignation our frail weak nature would afford but not with the Resignation of Job / I think I may truly say they were the Lords children they were such as would bring full grace to all Eternity - Their Tranquil Souls no longer dwell Within a tent of Clay Their flown to bliss in peaceful realms of everlasting Day!! Forgive this little heartfelt Effusion - but Oh! what is (?) that thou shouldest magnify "him" most Happy should I have been to have stopt here without pouring out to you any further troubles but it pleased the Divine Ruler who seeth not as Man will - to afflict us still further - our poor little Baby the dear little pledge of my Dear departed Celia did not survive her lamented Mother some 7 months - Yes my dear little "Celia Alice" has gone to join her sainted Parent in the regions of bliss where trouble and affliction cannot enter nor can the ungodly approach to disturb her repose - This little verse I would beg add and forgive my humble attempt at Poetry

> Dear Celia she has wing'd her flight
> to the pure realmns of endless light
> She sits adorned with every grace
> And views her Saviour face to face

You wish to know what Public ammusements we have in Sydney - You will be surprised when I tell you we have not one not even so much as a Public Ball or Assembly - I assure you my Dr. Cousin our ears are not assailed by any of the Wanton or corrupting airs of the opera no nor the majestic and ennobling melody of the Oratorio but they are frequently assailed with the noise of intoxicated People and the disgusting language of the Aborigine - The Winter generally passes away with but one or two Balls and when sweltering(?) summer arrives there are very frequently 4 and 5 in succession sometimes the "(?) Sheriff" entertains a numerous asssemblage of fashionables when the "Interesting Mrs. Abel" makes her appearance / sometimes our gay Naval Officer entertains his friends/ sometimes the "Atorney(?) General" or "the Chief Justice", "the Commissioner of the Court of Requests(?)" or the "Cashier of the Bank" ~ & & & I really cannot Imagine why they should give the prefrence to the summer unless it is for the sake of the fruits which grow so much more abundantly than in Winter / but as to the Eligibility of it I think I should not presume to offer an opinion as I never enter into Society except a few friends who we sometimes dine with or spend the Evening - Our principal ammusement is that of spending a few hours in the Boat of an afternoon I sometimes take my Book and sit on a Rock by the Water side to read while the others employ themselves with eating Oysters which we gather from the Rocks ourselves my Mother, Elizabeth & cousin Eliza very frequently accompany us and Generally one or two of our real friends who might sans ceremonie step in and dine with us/ I assure you My Dr. Cousin I feel much more pleasure in these little excursions than I should in any of their (?) assemblies / we generally take a little Bread and Butter in the Boat with us and when we go <u>for</u> <u>all</u> <u>day</u> we provide a cold Dinner/I sometimes collect Insects but I xxxxxx I cannot (as was my intention) complete a Box for you / however should it be in my power I will as I have no doubt you would prize them on account of being collected by the hands of your "unknown friend and Cousin" most happy should I be could you at any time join our happy little group -

I think I have been rather tardy in acknowledging the receipt of your pretty little present *(?) (?)* which I assure you was very much admired and for which I have to. return you my most cordial thanks —

This letter I am ashamed to say is not fit to go out of my hands at any rate such a distance but as I am aware it will meet no other than <u>Mr Hopes</u> I am not so uneasy / it is not bad writing alone that it is famed for but diction and <u>orthography</u> I trust he will excuse it / this day Elizabeth and Eliza came over to see me and they were so full of life and gaiety that I really could not write they pleased me so with their jokes that I scarcely knew what I was about I I was therefore obliged at last to leave my pen and have again about Ten Minutes ago resumed it - Tis now exactly 11 oclock and I have to send this off to night as the Mangles sails early to morrow morning therefore I must bid you Adieu and believe me to be yours with the greatest affection

<u>Jane</u> <u>Atkinson</u> - should your Brothers Sister or any friend enquire after me pray present my kind regards to them Mr A - Miss A - join me in Kind remembrances to you though perfectly unknown / Good night my Dear Cousin May every blessing attend you is the sincere wish of

J P A

Letter 11

The importance of this letter of Mary Reibey lies in the factual source material of conditions of her family lifestyle as of 1825, of her business connections with her cousin. Apart from the Travel notes (So called Diary) and the copies of two letters brought back in 1982 from Devon these other letters were not available in Australia until purchased by the Mitchell Library in the mid 1980s.

Mary Reibey is writing from Sydney in 1825 to Cousin David Hope She has suffered the deaths of two children and that of a baby granddaughter. This indomitable woman has picked up the threads of life in the Colony, busy with her overseas business, sending £100 sterling, the second of two such bills. Her eldest son Thomas Haydock Reibey II, while conquering his grieving for his loved sister, Celia, is returning to Entally, Tasmania, together with his young family, wife Richarda and children Mary, Thomas III and James. Note they had rested (along with three servants) with his mother our Mary Reibey in Sydney. This was possibly in the George Street North Home ... Pencilville at Newtown not yet mentioned. The large house Entally in Macquarie Place was let to the Bank of new South Wales ..at a rental of £ 160 per annum. Mary writes:

> how many do you think I have inmates of my House then / why their is Mrs Thomson (daughter Eliza) and her Two children and servants and Daughter Elizabeth and mostly my sisters daughter Ellza (FOSTER) and with my three servants we have a pretty good house…

It is, remember, the Letter of a woman emancipist carrying on her business.

Sydney June 19th 1825

My dear Cousin,

I merely write you a short Epistle to say we are very well and another separation is going to take place with part of my family / I told you in my last, of them all comeing up on a visit to Sydney and Thomas going to sea for the benefit of his Health he is now returned and is greatly recovered from his complaint which was in great measure a lowness of Spirit caused by the loss of his sister J Bn who was his delight, those Two above anything on this earth I think his whole soul where Centered in. he is now going down to Port Dalrymple where his Farms and Stock are with his family who as been stoping with me during his absence for six months consisting of wife 3 children and Three servants / the embark the day after tomorrow God send them safe to their desire homes, well then after dispatching them off how many do you think I have inmates of my House then / why their is my second son James and his wife their is Mrs Thomson and her Two children and servants / myself and daughter Elizabeth and mostly my sisters daughter Eliza and with my 3 servants we have a pretty good housefull / we also expect Mr & Mrs Atkinson to stop with us a week or two shortly till their House is finished but my House is pretty large / its capable of holding as many more it keeps me pretty busy. I have sent you by Capt McKellan 17 Sydney Gazzette from Nos 1109 to 1125 of our weekly Express from No 1 to 7 27 of the Australian from No 1 to to 36, 1 Australian Agricultural Compy for 1824 - the minitures are not done / I am afraid I shall not be able to get them done for some time as we have only man here that is clever and he is almost in a state of enibriety / I have begun a long letter to you which will be forwarded to you by the ship Phenix and which I daresay you will receive before this it will inclose the first of a bill of exchange on the Lords of the Treasury for £100 stg and the 2nd of of the one sent by the ship Hope Capt Norris for £100 Stg I hope you are in possesion of before now / I am very anxious for letters from you now it being time we should have receipts for £308-12-4 sent at different times before this / I must now conclude I am afraid I shall be too late to get them on Board from

Your ever affectionate Cousin

M.Reibey

They all desire their love
and Respects

Letter 12

This is the interesting letter from Daughter Eliza Thomson, married to that young Lieutenant who so assiduously squired the Reibey trio in London, returning with them to Sydney in 1821 in the Mariner. She, having holidayed in the UK writes to her cousin David Hope as an intimate family member. This Letter is dated July 24 (altered to 1825) from Sydney to Glasgow. Her grief for her siblings is expressed in typical 19th century century letter communication. All Mary's children are deeply imbued with Victorian sentiments. All were sincere. In this letter we get a glimpse of the very deep affection Ellza had for her husband. He was weak and became an embezzeller of his government trust funds. All the family, in their letters, speak poorly of him. Yet they stood by the man, repaying the lost money to save him from whatever fate the courts would have decreed. All this lay ahead of them. It warms one to know that his wife was so fond of him; she writes:

> no one can imagine how much I am suffering owing to this short absence from my beloved husband / I feel that this world would be a blank without him / he is a kind and affectionate partner.

Deal Ship Letter
Glasgow 23 Dec 1825

To David Hope

Sydney July 6th 1824 *(altered to 1825)*

My Dear Cousin

It is so long since I have had the pleasure of receiving letter from you that I do not knew whether to say you have forgotten me or not, however I will be like the merciful Judge and not condemn you but attribute it not to want of affection towards me but merely because you do not think it any consequence to write to a "<u>wee bit body</u>" like Cousin Eliza, now is not this this the case? but now I will so far condesend no to make an apology to you, for my long silence and I hope when my dear Cousin understands why it had been so long he will pardon it, of course you will have heard all the particulars of our late melancholy and severe loss, and I am sure my Cousin will not be surprized at my not writing him when I assure him that ever since that fatal event, my heart has been too sad almost to write to any one, particularly one I am connected with for I am aware that when writing to a Relation I must nesesarily mention what I would most willingly avoid for whenever it is mentioned it seems as though my wounds bleed afress, not that it is ever out of my thought no, night and day and every hour it dwells upon my mind, I am sure my Friend will enter into all my feelings on such a Subject, it is one that my immagination never led me to suppose would fall to my lot to record, oh little did I think when I gave my Sister the last Embrace when I was leaving Sydney that it would be the last time in this world that I should hold so beloved and affectionate a relative to my heart, and that her days where numbered to so short a span, that that lovely form was so soon to mingle with her kindred dust, so soon be numbered with the dead: so soon to lay down her head in the Grave, she drooped like a beautious Flower, that for a short time spread a fragrance around, and before the Evening Sun goes down, droops whithers, and dies, but she died in the Faith of her Redeemer never once did she repine, she used to say "do not weep but pray for me the Lords will be done", she might have exclaimed, "oh Death where is thy sting" she bore all her sufferings like an Angel for all that was excellent in Woman was comprised in that form, My beloved Brother too, his youthful head was soon laid where the the "Wicked cease from troubling and the weary are at rest" he was only just entering into the world ignorant of its wickedness unacquainted with vice, and so soon to be cut off, oh my dear Cousin these where heavy afflictions, but shall such frail mortals as we are murmur or repine at the Almightys will, it was him that did the deed, and shall we dare to ask his reason, he has wise reasons for all his actions. - I attended my dear Brothers death bed, and never never may I again endure such another trial it was almost too much for my poor heart, to see him I loved so tirelesly, laying in an agony of pain, and not a word of Complaint escape his lips, he bore all his sufferings with the greatest patience and appeared to be perfectly resigned, but when he resigned his breath he appeared to have fallen into a sweet sleep, so gentle and without a groan did he leave this world of woe, and then so soon to follow the Death of my departed Sisters Infant, it seemed as though it had only been born to be regretted, so perfect a little Angel it was, but oh it was only a blossom. bloomed to fall so soon, its innocent spirit fled this Earth and joined its Sainted Mother in realms of perfect bliss. I must not dwell on these Melancholy Subjects any longer for my heart is full. - I am now up in Sydney spending two or three months with my Mother who I am happy to say enjoys very Good health, I came up for the purpose of seeing her, as well as getting an operation performed on Mary Hs Hands for when she was scalded,through neglect they became con-pacted, and I have now had them cut, and I have no doubt it will be an excellent cure / she is very well in her health, indeed we all*(?)* expected when they where cut she would be *(?)* *(?)* and be reduced very much but instead of that she is getting *(?)* stout, I have now got a little Boy just ten months old, and a remarkably stout Child and very healthy / I can assure you his Papa is not a little proud of him, he does not think there is such another Boy in the World as his, When I last heard from my dear Husband he was quite well and very anxious for my return and I can assure you I am not a little anxious to Embrace him that all my happiness *(?)* with, no one can imagine how much I am suffering owing this short absence from my beloved Husband / I feel that this world would be a blank without him, he is a kind and affectionate partner, nay I do not Envy the greatest and the Richest in the world. with such a being as it has been my happiness to be united to, and I hope my dear Cousin when it falls to your lot you will enjoy as much happiness in the Married State as has fallen to my share. Remember me to all Friends that enquire for me, the Cochranes, Mr Grahame, Mr and Mrs Fleming,and when you go to Edinburgh remember me to Miss Duncan, and the Robertsons and the Reochs. I have written to Margaret Reoch this time, when Mr Thomson last heard from Capt Wood he was quite well, We hear from him almost every week, he has built a very fine House, but he still says he wants a Wife, give my kind regards to that Family

do not forget to remember me very kindly to your Mary tell her I I have not forgot her and never shall, and do not call me selfish when I often say I wish I had so valuable a creature for this is a wretched Country for Servants,I often talk about her and wish I had such a one here / tell her I often often think of her kindly. When you write your Brother and Sister give my love to them and tell your Sister I shall write her as soon as I return home but my mind is so unsettled I cannot at present. I am affraid you will think this a sad scrawl but the ship sails very early in the morning and this must go to my (?) and Mother has been calling me to make haste for this last half hour, : must therefore conclude and accept of my love and beleive me to remain

your affectionate Cousin

Eliza Thomsom

A note was added in pencil after the letter had been opened, about a certain D.W. suffering persecution on account of his religious principles.

Letter 13

From Mary Reibey in Sydney to Cousin David Hope Glasgow Dated August 5 1825.

Again the merchant lady writer of her business affairs, transfer of monies, expense of shipping at £3 per ton and so on Then we read the little snippets about the family. She confirms the Thomson Couple's happy marriage. Likewise the return to Entally, Tasmania, of Thomas Reibey II with his little family... No less than fifteen days to sail from Sydney to Tasmania. Incredible when compared to today's Sydney to Hobart Yacht Race. Her description of the immigrants in their variety is interesting: ironic also her vinegary remarks about 'the most depraved Convicts'. We know Mary Reibey spent much of her time with Church matters. The Rev McArthur now of Sydney, is aping the great Dr Chalmers of Glasgow, with his hoarse oratory. She speaks of miniatures being painted of her children which she, Mary, hopes herself to carry to England. Anticipating this possibility, but not certainty, she hopes to bring the youngest girl, Elizabeth with her to visit for perhaps three years. Again her old Nurse and husband are remembered with a five pound note These two were the only people from 1790, who recognised her on her return to Blackburn and Bury in 1820. One feels the conflicting ties between her native country and her real home, New South Wales. Mary is still troubled with Asthma which plagued her throughout her adult life.

Per Pheonix
Deal
Post marked Glasgow 23 Dec 1825

Sydney August 5 1825

My dear Cousin

through the Ship Phoenix returning to this Port Consequently has brought the letters and small packet of newspapers back I had sent to you by her/and in addition to the papers I have sent 5 Sydney Gazzettes from 1128 to 1133 5 of Hoares Express from No 9 to 14 5 Australian from no 38 to 43. The Cash is the same namely the first of a bill of exchange on the Lords of the Treasury and 2nd of bill sent by Broadfoot each for £100 Stg / the accounts one not yet brought to a close I mentioned in my letter of date July 5th of the Carpeting being left at the Derwent and stored at Bethmu(?) and Grants, I accordingly wrote them to sell for the best prices could be got and inclosed them the Invoice that came in your- letter / I think theire must be a letter of advice but that has not come to hand yet but they had reshiped them on board ' the Brig Nexus bound for Port dalrymple at £3 per ton and it is expected she will be a month or six weeks/so you see, through theire mistake it may make a material difference in the Market and expences / I shall not open those Bales,/ Mrs Thomson is still with me and very anxious to return / Mr T. has written her he is quite tired of being alone I think he will never let her come again without himself,/I got a letter from my son Thomas that they all got down safe and fifteen days passage, / their is a young man here by the name of Anderson that Mr Reach (?) gave a letter of introduction Recomending him strongly/I think he said he was a ministers son/I asked him and Mr Wallace to dine with us which they did and I gave them a General invitation but I never saw either of them with the exception of Mr Wallace/Called one day after when I was very ill, I believe him to be a decent young man / Mr Anderson got a situation in Mr Wentworths office the Barrister who wrote the History of N.S.W. which place he soon left through his incapacity as Mr W. said to fill the situation / I was very much afraid he will do no good here I reed a note from him the other day praying my assistance he being then confined in Goal for the sum of £5.0.0 at the suit of Cuningham the Ship Builders from Leith/I was going to liberate him immeadiatly but a thought struck me to write to Cuningham Concerning him / he sent back for answer Anderson had letters to him from his friends in Leith and in Consequence paid him all the attention in his power and after that lent him £5.0.0 which he had every reason to suppose was not aplied to the best of purposes/Consequently I declined (?) it / I then recd another note from him saying that Cuningham had agreed to take his note for a month providing he would pay costs which was 40/-/I immeadiately sent him that sum he promised my servant he whd. call on me the next morning after he was out but I understand since it was nothing but a stratagem to get a little money to spend in disapation/I am told he is a worthless Charracter for which I am very sorry as I know Mr Reach(?) will be vexed he gave him a letter / when my servant took the Money to the goal he was the bearer of another note from that Davis you gave the memo. to,/the Charracter before I did not send him any thing but I sent to his wife relief who I belive is very badly off / a number of these Emigrants come out and spend what little Cash they have before the offer to do anything for their future prospects the generaly turn out very bad, their are a great many of them so bad or worse than the most depraved Convicts the go about swindling any one they can lay hold of we have instances of it every day with us/

Mr McArthur is now up on a visit to Sydney I suppose to meet the Arch Deacon to come in for a share of the Church lands, theire is great alterations here now with the Clergy since his arrival we have heard him Mr McArthur several times / I think he is atempting to Tread in Dr Chalmers steps/ he Certainly is a very Clever man and I think a very good one / he is now liveing at Mr Wemyss the Commissary he called on Eliza Twice/ he expects going down to the Derwent at the time Eliza goes / he is rather too voilent in the pulpit I am afraid it will Ingure his lungs —we are now dayly expecting our new Governor and the Seretary / I suppose their will be great alterations in our Government but tis all the same to me / I never meddle in polatics / you will see by the papers they are discussing the busness between Dr Douglas and the Revd. I Marsden / tis said that neither perty can make good their aspertions and that Douglas will get his situation as Clerk to the Council with a Salary of 800 per annum/ I think I shall be able to let you have the minitures now very shortly / we have got I am told a very Clever man now / Eliza and James is now sitting as they are going down so soon / I shall then be able to judge if he does them well / if so James and Elizabeth will be the next and what whd you say if I where to be the bearer of them myself / if I do come it will be all in a hurry when I have fixed upon it / I do not say I am in earnest but I feel very much inclined / I shall bring Elizabeth with me she is growing the picture of her sister Celia both in figure and every thing I think she is just her height / if we do come we shall stay a few years - poor Mr Wills is just getting into the same way as Celia I think he will soon follow her if he does not very soon take a turn, he is a very fine young man he goes up the Country tomorrow morning to Mr Refesnes(?) his Brother-in-law(?) who is a surgeon and I think the change of air may be of service/ I have been packing his things up he says he think he never will be able to come down again alive / the Miss Atkinson and sister to Janes Husband was on Teusday last Married to Capt John Grimes a Native of this Colony / I think it is a good match for her when she came out I understood or it was rather given out she had an engagement in England but as it will tis all over now / the sail tomorrow morning for the Ile of France for sugars & - I inquired about that man Murdock and find / by a servant Maid of Mrs Atkinson who lived sometime in the same place / stays(?) at Mr Oxleys as Cook & his wife as Housekeeper/I coud not find out what he left Mr Murdock for, I expect long ere this you have been Mr Lang the Minister/ he has lost his Brother since his departure a very fine and worthy young man,/as for Mr Warren I cannot say anything about as I belive he is now on a Ship to Newcastle & I had liked to have forgot I wrote to Alice by this Conveyance and I desired her to say to you I wished you whould (if they are alive my old Nurse & her Husband) pay over to them £5.0.0 from that Money (£60.0.0) you have of mine in the Bank and the rest you may send out in a little investment of which I had advised you

I see you are about removing to a larger establishment it is a good sign and believe me I am as anxious about your prosperity as you can possible be and may you many years continue to have your health which is more prescious than Rubys, to you or any one else I hope you will take care of it/ some times Relapses one worse than the first atack / I have had some very bad atacks lately of the Astma or with that exat(?) I think I should enjoy a tolerable(?) state of health but never I am afraid I shall be the woman I was Two years ago - I must now beg of you to present my kind compliments to Mr & Mrs Fleming and all inquiring friends Eliza sends her Dear love to you in which Betsy joins remember us all to Mr Cockran and all the young Ladies / I long to be with you again / Mrs. Atkinson also presents her love to you from

your ever affectionate Cousin

M. Reibey

Letter 14

From James H Reibey, son of Mary. Launceston, Van Diemans Land August 10th 1829. to David Hope, Glasgow.

In this letter to his Cousin David, James deals with important happenings. We learn about the pirating of the Eclipse, the murder of his Uncle Foster, the imprisonment of Lieut . Thomson and the weddings of his sisters: his own business worries and the failed sale of expensive carpeting, therefore the delayed remittance to Glasgow; his own illness; his mother's distress at the stalled cash flow. This largely, so James claims, due to the family rescue of brother-in-law Thomson, mainly by Thomas Reibey II, James and Mary Reibey. In this letter we hear the full facts of Thomson's larceny. James writes of The living -above- his needs, Thomson's slackness in his accounting; his imprisonment and the seizure of all the Thomson property by the injured Government; and the troubled family. Yet Mary is visiting all the family groups in Launceston and Entally at Hadspen and will return to Sydney in James' own vessel, the Hetty. Here is an account of Elizabeth's wedding to Lieutenant Innes. Their son Long Innes and grandson became notable in the legal profession. James describes this union as a love match but not as solid as he would have liked. Sister Eliza's children, despite their father's troubles are marrying with varied success, in worldly terms. The interesting murder of his uncle Foster is summarily dealt with.

> you know old Foster was found dead ,supposed to be murdered, as he was on the way from the interior of New South Wales to give evidence against some cattle stealers.

The Eclipse was a vessel belonging to two of them, James Reibey and John Atkinson, leased to the Government to carry coal from Newcastle to Sydney. James reminds David Hope of the need to pursue Sir Thomas Brisbane on his return from New South Wales to Britain; The retiring Governor having promised to ask for compensation for the loss of the Eclipse. As James points out:

> our loss was more glaring as the Vessel was taken from the Port of Newcastle in the open day moored close to the Wharf, and within Pistol Shot of the Centinel On duty by the very Men *(Convicts)* in Government Employ to load her *(with coals)* which Cargo was purchased by us paying them 10/- per ton for them and for which they were to put them on board /and these men were the Pirates, overpowering the Crew and taking her out of the Harbour having the wind and the tide on their favour and the Govt. Not a boat to send after her...

Since the Campbells having suffered a similar loss had been compensated with land, (in fact Duntroon in the ACT) James stresses they are happy to attract similar compo. if, he adds:

> they will not give us Cash in remuneration. Land would do at at a fair valuation in part if not for the whole.

Truly one of the most interesting letters in this Collection.

Launceston Van Diemans
Land August 10th 1829

Dear Cousin

Your much esteemed favor of the 8th November last is now before me in which you refer me to yours pr. William Young of the 6th Ult./this letter I duly received and as there was a vessel just weighing Anchor for Sydney at the Moment I received it I enclosed it to my Mother with a request it might be returned to me/ My Mother shortly after arrived here (is here now) and forgot to bring your letter with her or I certainly should have answered it by the last ship, but you must recollect we live in a very out of the way place in the far extreme of the Island to where Hobart Town is situate and therefore seldom know exactly when a ship sails/ your charge against me for discontinuing writing you is quite just and I take great shame to myself and in fact you you must be very good to look over my neglect, the only apology I can offer is that I never understood to the Contrary but that but that my Mother was in constant corespondence with you untill she arrived here about two Months ago,/and for these last Six Months I have been very ill for some time my life was completely despaired of / I had a severe attack of Inflamation in the bowels and three Doctors who attended me gave me up,/ I certainly recovered by a Miracle, this must plead my excuse for some months but had I known my Mother had not written you for some time I certainly would have written you a few lines occasionaly to inform you how we were getting on / another cause of my not writing you before was in consequence of the harrassed state of my mind for the very blameable and foolish conduct of Thomson, l the event has justified my forebodings, entrusted as he was, at the head of Customs & Treasury of this part of the Island with immence Sums of Money with a Salary of only £300 per Annum to be careless so as hardly to keep any accounts and to live at the rate of £800 or 900 pr. Year/ all my advice and knowledge only served to irritate and make him shun my society / the Consequence is that Govt. at last took notice of it, every thing he had was Seized (all the property Mrs T. had from my Mother included) and sold and he thrown into Prison, the deficiency was about £3,000. My Brother Thomas and Myself had at last come forward to save him from a worse fate (as was threatened) and became security for the Amount to Government, which released him,/ his property has paid off about one half and there may still be some errors which it is supposed will be but I am affaid we shall have to pay about £1000 independent of this/ My Mother has assisted and paid in Cash for them about £2,000, some of his Bills which My Mother endorsed have lately come back on her, they were drawn on his Uncle Young's of Burnt island, this has much injured my Mother in taking up, as they came suddenly upon her,/ this I believe has prevented her as much as anything remitting some money she owes you she is continually talking about it & you and saying she is ashamed to write you / I was trying very much the other day to get her a Bill on England for £100 to remit you but could not succeed for her / Mr & Mrs Thomson are living on their farm at Pattersons Plains but Ill off and he is so very lazy and useless a being that he cannot turn his hand to anything,/ I have no patience with him so extravagant and so careless, and to add to their misfortune Mrs T. has just been confined of her fifth child,/ his Uncle John seem inclined not to do anything for him / they ought after My Mother has embarrassed her affairs for some time in I may say foolishly paying Money for him.

My Mother some time back sent me a bale of Carpetting one that came by your recommendation from some part of Scotland,/ this Carpetting I sold here on Credit to a shopkeeper of the name of Ash, he shortly after failed, and having a good opinion of the Young Man and willing to assist him I advanced him large sums of money and became security for other sums including my former debt Carpetting included of about £1,500/ he repaid me some part of the Cash advances I had made him, when unfortunately he was killed from a fall off a horse, leaving me Minus Carpetting included of £870. I seized on all his property I could get hold of on this side and a Lawyer of the name of Butler at Hobart Town seized on all he could get hold off/ and as the accident happened then he had the start of me, this Butler was his Guardian and has advanced a claim on him for some English outlays as he states before their arrival in this Colony,/ we are at law(?) now who will obtain Letters of Administration from the Supreme Court, but the little property left is hardly worth while contending for, and if I succeed the whole probably will be swallowed up in law expences. I am extremely sorry to have to send you such an account of the Carpetting. I would have communicated to you before respecting it but was in hope of something better turning up.

My Mother as I stated before is here / Mrs Atkinson is also who accompanied my Mother down / they go up in a few days in a vessel of mine the Hetty to Sydney again. You will probably hear before this <u>My Sister Elizabeth's Marriage</u> about three Months ago at Sydney to a <u>Lieutenant Innes</u>

of the 39th Regiment who is also adjutant. I have not seen him but I understand he is a very fine Young Man and highly respected,he was brought up at the Military College,/ it was as it appears quite a Love Match but my Mother has settled £200 per Year on her and her heirs as well as a farm at present let for 70£ more and an improving property - I have just received a letter from her by a vessel arrived this Evening from Sydney / she seems very happy and gay, but I would sooner have seen her married to a steady sober farmer or Citizen,/ Atkinson is not doing very well he has had some expected claims from England on him lately, but he has industry and perseverence,/ you know long ere this that Eliza Foster was married to a Mr Pitman an American Gentleman from China, extremely well off and a most exellent man, but I do not expect she will live long as she is in a deep consumption -/ Mrs Foster her Mother lives with them and she has a good farm and some other property of her own, you know old Foster was found dead supposed to be murdered as he was on the way from the interior of New South Wales to give evidence against some Cattle stealers - the eldest daughter Jane was some years ago married to a man of the name of Patten (formerly Master of a vessel)/ they keep a Public House in this Town and he has turned out a drunken beast / she is very steady and they are well off,/ it was an unhappy circumstance for our family they ever came here/ we have never been so united since/ she (Mrs F) is a perfect D——l -

I send you accompanying this a letter some time back written to Messrs Young the owners of the North Britain & Wm. Young respecting a difference that has occured between myself and their drunken Agent a Mr Morrisson of Sydney. When Read please send it to them sealed if you think I am right in so doing, I pledge myself to the truth of every sentence -

Your Communication with Sir Thomas Brisbane respecting the Eclipse I am exceedingly obliged for and I am sure Atkinson will be the same when he Knows of it,/ I am astonished at Sir Thomas' Neglect, he promised me most faithfully personally in Sydney he would get us Remuneration for the Loss. I gave him all the Certificates and documents relating thereto at his own Request previous to his departure from New South Wales, I also wrote him a long letter eighteen months ago reminding him of his promise and recapitulating the whole of the story again on purpose to assist his memory/ I have not heard from him since/he is a good man but very forgetful, his loss is much felt in these Colonies, I see he has acknowledged the receipt of the additional documents sent home by Mr Atkinson, and I hope you will not let him rest untill he has done something for us to redeem his pledge / his last words to me were,

"I feel for the loss you & Mr Atkinson has sustained severely had there been a precedent in the Colony I would order you immediate remuneration, but if you will extract me with the documents as I am about leaving N.S.W. for England I pledge myself I will use all my endeavours to get you some recompence"

at that time I could not find a precedent, but it was after-wards found in the Case of the Boy Harrington Captain Campbell and which was the substance of the additional documents sent home by Mr Atkinson,/ our loss was also more glaring, as the Vessel was taken away from the Port *(Newcastle)* in the open day moored close to the Wharf, and within Pistol Shot of the Centinel on duty by the very Men *(Convicts)* in Government Employ employed to load her *(with Coals)* which Cargo was purchased by us from the Government paying them 10/- per ton for them and for which they were to put them on board,/ and these men so employed by them (the Govt) were the Pirates, overpowering the Crew and taking her out of the harbour having the Wind and Tide in their favor as (?) (?) any in the Port and the Govt not a boat to send after her —— I know your disposition so well you will leave no stone unturned to gain Atkinson and Myself a recompense,/ our value of the vessel was £1,600, after she was taken away/ Sir Thomas ordered the Master attendant to Value her, but he not knowing the stores &c she had on board valued her very low at £1,000 or £1,100 I forget which, but this Certificate of Valuation was given with the other documents to Sir Thomas/ if they will not give us Cash in remuneration Land would do at a fair valuation in part if not for the whole

My Brother Thomas & family are quite well he has still but <u>three</u> <u>Children</u> he is very industrious and is one of the first farmers and Graziers in this Island,/ he has nearly twelve thousand acres of land - Mother & Mrs Atkinson are at present at Mr Thomsons four miles from Town / I Remain yours most truly and faithfully obliged Cousin

Mr D. Hope, Glasgow

James H. Reibey

Letter 15

*M*ary *Reibey through one of her few preserved letters, dated Sydney October 20th 1829, is once more discovered pursuing business interests with her Dear Cousin, David Hope of Glasgow.*

Her records seem meticulouos so far as her correspondence is concerned.She discusses various monies and some of her ventures.Mary has indeed endeavoured to sponsor a Chemist..."a Chymist & Druggist".. but the long delay with supplies has cancelled out that project... others have set up pharmacies. Things are bad, that is money ventures,in the Colony in 1829,

> their is no money the the Colony noone will buy under 12 or 18 months credit here and their is a question wether the bills are good

and so on. She tells of Mr Thomson's indebtedness,

> they *(Govt.)* have already taken from him indeed every head of cattle and...grains of wheat he had. I am afraid he is as Idle as ever/ my poor Eliza has now got 5 Children...

She had generously given Elizabeth, upon her marriage to Lt Innes, (39th Rgt) a farm and £200 per annum ,

> which with his pay will support them very handsome

Indeed we have a letter here covering all business and a bare bones account of the family as at 1829.

per ship Harmony

India Letter, Portsmouth - 20th Oct 1829 (Recd)

Sydney October 20th 1829

to Mr David Hope Glasgow

My dear Cousin I have lately received a letter from Mssrs Gregory Thomson & Co Kilmarnock Concerning the goods sent me appointing Mr How to settle them / be assured I am extreamly glad - has it as been a source of vexation and trouble to me and no doubt they will think I have not acted right with them, but I hope as soon as Mr H can sit down with me he will be able to convince them and you I have done my best / the state the Colony has been in these last three years has rendered impossible for any one to make good their acccounts, you complain loudly of my not writeing - there may may be some Cause but not quite so bad as you of course must think, as I understand you have not received any letters since Jany 1827 No 21 / so Mr How said you told him and which I immediately referred to my Book and showed him dates 19 June 1828 No 22 by the Megonet*(?)* bound for Glasgow / 28 Oct 1828 by Mrs Wemyss our late Commissarys Lady with a parcell for Mrs Irvin Containg Two India Crepe Gown pieces, one for Williams Wife and which I am Certain will deliver safe / if She arrives well the next the 3d of Jan 1829 by the Hellen through Mr Morrison, 29 Jany 29/20th March Capt Doughty ship Eliza by which I sent twenty one 21 Bales of Wool to Acct of those bills I drew on your House for £602.18.10 / I have also remitted the first and second of Treasury bills for £250 as also the first of one hundred pounds / the second I now transmit altho a lapse of time has transpired since remitting the first but their being no opportunity before I had included it when I was at the southward to send by the Alice but was not in time for the post but I hope & Trust you have long ere this recvd the first, the Wool I bought on speculation namely for a remittance at 1/ one shilling a pound sterling the nett Amount was £255.5.10 / knowing it was a good sample I hope it will pay me but I know you will do your best for me.

I now enter into family affairs which to you O I had liked to have forgot for I must tell you all my Busness affairs / I wrote Mr Hargreaves about Two years & half ago to send out a little medicin to set up a person as Chymist & Druggist who had been in that line in England and who was about takeing one of my Houses / of course the man had everything to arrange in his House and the fitting up cost him a deal of money / he also detained Two young men in his service to dispence them till it nearly ruined him expecting they whould come in due course / but Ship after Ship arrived and no investment the Young men where obliged to seek other employment and he Mr Colhist(?) had to let part of his House to assist in paying his rent having given up all thoughts of them comeing out, indeed we both had written him not to send them as it had been such a lengthy time / in the, meantime out comes a person from London of the name of Foss and set up and has amassed quite a fortune - now the Country is quite full of them, had Mr Hargreaves sent them out within 15 or 18 months Mr Colhist whould have had no. oponent and might equally done as well as Foss but after the lapse of nearly Two years and half out comes an Invoice over of £908.0 / Mr. Colhist will not take them having made Arrangt otherwise Consequently they are thrown all on my hands they are now lying in Mr Pitmans stores / I have had the first legal advice in the Colony and they say they are of the Opinion that I can refuse to receive them after such a length of time but unfortunately I was down at Launceston when they arrived and they where lodged in Mr Pitmans Stores as my Agent. I really do not know what to do with them their is no money in the Colony no one will buy under 12 or 18 months credit here and their is a question wether the bills are good / they also say the goods are laid in at much too high prices their are similar Invoices in the Country which are from 50 to 75 per cent Cheaper/ I think of reshipping them again but I should like if I could Sell it all at a small loss to do the best I can for him but at present I see no likelihood / I had desired him to buy me a small Carriage that he did not send nor do I wish he whould as every Article here now is much below prime cost or mostly so, owing to the scarcity of Money / I wrote Mr H. about 7 or 8 months ago not to send it nor the medicin I suppose he must have shipped them before he received my letter / I have got all this Trouble through my own good nature to some others.

I suppose you will be tired of this complaint, so I must just give you the last occurances of my family I believe I wrote you about Mr. Thomson since I have been down to the southward and did all in my power to settle his busness / their appeared in his Accts when I was down their an error of £9 or £1100 which was sent over to Hobart Town for the Commissioners to examine / the result I have not heard yet as I left before they came over but if that is the case will lesson the debt or near pay it of with what they have already taken from him / indeed every head of cattle and my Grains of Wheat he had / I am afraid he is as Idle as ever my poor Eliza has now got five 5 children it is for such a young Creature a miserable prospect / to besure he is very kind and affectionate to her but that is not all, as I tell him it wants his exertions and activity to support such a family / she is quite a slave to them it whould delight you to see her children with what order and neatness she keeps them had she a Husband equal to herself they might have been amongst the first people in the Colony but he is fit for nothing / I do no know any one thing he can do for the Farm he now lives on he quite neglects but I hope he will soon see his error I have talked to him seriously,

I did not write you about Elizabeths marriage / She was married about six months ago to a Lieutenant Innes adjutant of the 39th Regt. a very fine young man is only 6 foot 7 inches high and I think will make her a very good Husband / I have settled upon her £200 a year besides her Farm with his pay which is about the same will support them very handsome with occonomy, he is a very clever young man and an exellent Correspondent / She Elizabeth wrote you some time back thanking you for the handsome present you sent her did you receive it She desired me to give her kind regards to you and accept my best wishes for your health (which I hope is quite restored)

and happyness from your affectionate Cousin

M.Reibey

As please to give my love John & wife & little Penelope, William and wife and ask the latter if she

received the crepe gown through Mrs Irvin

love to Alice and her spouse & little George

Letter 16

Letter from son-in-law, John Atkinson of Sydney NSW 8th Sept; 1830 to David Hope of Glasgow.
This short letter relates to the pirated Eclipse..see earlier letters. Interpreting the information in this letter: he has included the official affidavits from such important witnesses as the Master of the Cutter.

> ... remember that the crew were overpowered, bound and apparently left behind *(on the wharf?)* with the outwitted Government Centinels -

these papers then, were not taken earlier as believed, to England to present to the Colonial Office. It appears in fact the documents have just been rediscovered in the Secretary's office .

One could be forgiven for murmuring 'What's new , Pussycat?"

In fact Mr John Atkinson has submitted a very business like list of witnesses and character references for his cousin to offer a commission to Nessrs Buckles & Co to pursue the matter of compensation.

This is the only surviving, (1992) letter from the spouses of Mary's children. She has already written very happily of her relations with John Atkinson.

India Letter Deal
Glasgow 20 Feb 1831 (Recd)
Sydney New South Wales
8th Sept. 1830

Sir

From several letters I have recd. of late from my Brother in Law <u>J. H.</u> <u>Reibey</u> & also from my Father in London, I find that myself & Mr. R. are under very great obligations to you for the unending Exertions you have made to obtain for us a remuner(?) for the loss of <u>our</u> <u>Cutter</u>, which was piratically taken from Newcastle.

Being assured from the *(?)* Interest you take in the affair, that will again Aid us by your Friendly Interference / I have at the request Mr. Reibey forwarded to the Address Messrs Buckles, Bagster & Buckles of London agents to Mr Reibey the whole of the *(? — line of text missing)*

left in mistake by him, they were found the Secretarys Office lately -

The Instructions <u>Mr. Reibey</u> has given to Messrs Buckles & Co are

"to take charge of them until they hear from Mr Hope wether they are to send them to Scotland to him or deliver them to the Colonial Office at once"

I should judge that without doubt, it will be better for you to receive, inspect, & forward all, thro such means as you may consider most likely to bring the matter to a favorable conclusion

The papers forwarded to Messrs B & Co *(?)* as follows Viz

1. Affidavit of Mr C J Pound Master of the Eclipse
2. Statement of Captn Allman, Commandant at Newcastle / enclosed in Memo to Mr Reibey
3. Statement of Mr A Livingstone Master of the Lord Liverpool
4. Letter from Mr Campbell to Mr. Reibey
5. Valuation of Mr Nicholson / Master attendant of the vessel
6. Letter from Mr F S Forbes to Messrs R & A
7. Memorials-of R & A for compensation
8. Statement of particulars of Loss of Eclipse by R & A
9. Coln. Secretarys Letter to Mr R enclosing *???* Returning the above

Thanks for disinterested kindness, & relying in

full confidence of a favourable *(?)*

your unending perseverance

I Remain

Sir

Your much obliged

John Atkinson

to David Hope Esqr.

Glasgow

Letter 17

From James Reibey (son of Mary R.) from Launceston Van Diemens Land 18th April, 1832 to Messrs Fleming & Hope.Glasgow

This is a business letter from James which he enclosed with a family note, letter no 18. Again he refers to the unfortunate deal in carpeting and tapes.

He is adamant in pursuit of the Eclipse loss: compensation still being sought is here reviewed. Governor Darling is definitely not interested in any recompense other than;

the paltry gratuity of 600 Acre of Land jointly ...worth about 2/6
an Acre

James and John have sent further applications by Colonel Arthur to the U.K.and as we have read, copies to Buckles & Co through John Atkinson.
James concludes:

General Darling was the most Ferocious Tyrant that ever Governed
a Colony.

Recd 17.10.32
Launceston Van Diemens Land
18th. April 1832

Messrs Fleming & Hope
Glasgow

Gentlemen

I had the pleasure of addressing you in May last in reply to your favour of the 3rd Decr. 1830 and gave you the history of the Box of tapes as well as the Bale of Carpeting which I informed you had met with a most unfortunate fate in being sold and handed over to the late firm of Payne and Ash who some time afterwards failed and has not as yet paid one farthing to the Several Creditors and leaving me minus 800£,

Since this I have had the pleasure of receiving your favour of the 17th September last per Lord Byron wishing I would hand you an Account Sales of the Box of tapes which I should be most happy to do if there was any funds realised on them / suffice it to say that I had sold them at 40prs on the Invoice. I am however anxious that you should be no losers by the Circumstances and will be most happy to pay the Invoice price of the Box of tapes if that would be agreeable, a letter from you signyfying your approbation I will remit the amount / somewhere about 40 £ I think it was /

General Darling having positively refused to award any remuneration to Mr Atkinson and myself for the loss of the <u>Eclipse</u> we memorialed Lord Goderick on the subject sent one copy thro Lt. Govr. Arthur of this Island and another thro Genl. Darling. Some short time afterwards we where surprised by the receipt of a Letter from the Colonial Secretary of Sydney in the name of Genrl Darling ordering us the paltry gratuity of 600 Acre of Land jointly / it is worth about 2/6 an Acre. This was after Genl. Darling had left the Colony As the memorial was gone we backed it up with an explanatory Letter to Lord Goderick which we forwarded by Colonel Arthur and I am still in hopes that his Lordship will think it right to make us a more hansome Gratuity or Compensation or whatever they like to call it / all the original Papers are in Buckles & Co hands which Mr Atkinson sent home to you thro them and if you think it would be advisable for you to make another application on our behalf you had better make use of them. General Darling was the most Ferocius Tyrant that ever Governed a Colony / they think more favorably of General Bourke(?)

I Remain
Gentlemen
Your much obliged Servant
James H. Reibey

Letter 18

From James Reibey in Launceston 18th April 1832, enclosed with previous business Letter 17 to David Hope.

Marked Private.And James adjures priacy on all his information. No wonder .

This letter is indeed grist to the historian's mill. Information packed. Thomas Reibey II is planning a trip from Entally to England,where the wealthy Colonial will put his two young sons to school.The boys Tom III who later became feisty Archdeacon Reibey of Entally and later Tasmanian premier; and James III who became a Vicar of Denbury in Devon, grandfather of beautiful Charlotte (Reibey) William-Powlett. Dear loving wife Eliza Thomson now has six children. Many comments follow as to the continuing worthlessness of Mr Thomson... Elizabeth Innes together with her Lieut. move on with his regiment to India. Later, one does not know for fact, but understands that Elizabeth and her tribe made London a permanent residence in her sere and yellow. At any rate descendants live there now.As for his mother, Mary, he writes

she has turned Farmer in her old days/ she cultivates a Farm on
the Hawkesbury.

*Most interesting remembering Mary and Thomas I settled on his grant on the
Hawkesbury in 1794.*

*The Atkinsons mean to settle in Tasmania at Pattersons Plains. John Atkinson is
credited with industrious habits. Old Aunt Haydock Foster is around, making mantua/
mantles and bonnets. Her children's successes/ failures are dutifully reported to the
Scottish cousin.*

Private   Launceston 18th April 1852

Dear Cousin

My Brother and his Family are thinking to make a trip Home next year / he
wishes take his Children in order to place them at School in England

My Wife feels grateful for your kind expression in her favor contained in
your last Letter and hopes one of these days yet to have the pleasure of seeing
you. Mr and Mrs Thomson are well they have Six Children and are but poorly
off, he has not yet got quit of the Government Claims and as my Brother and
Self are bound for him, we have no Idea how it will end, he is the most lazy
fellow I ever met with in all the Course of my life / Mrs Pxxxxxxxxxx I have
not seen her since I received your last letter / Mr & Mrs Innes go on to India
with the Regt. about September next / they have two little Girls, My mother
is quite well the last time I heard, she has turned Farmer in her old days she
Cultivates a Farm on the Hawkesbury. Mr Atkinson was down here Shortly and
Intends to bring his Family down to Settle here at Pattersons Plains / they
are also but poorly of but he is Industrious and deserves to get on. This is
of course all private. Old Mrs Foster is now here she has a Farm and works
as a mantle(?) maker / the only good one of that Family was Eliza Mrs Pitman
and she poor thing was Cut off in her prime / Jane her eldest daughter is
married to a man of the name of Patten who keeps a Public House and who
uses her very ill / the Eldest son I have never seen but (?) he is also here
somewhere but I do not know what he is doing, James the Youngest is
Apprenticed to a Carpenter, / the old man you are aware was murdered in
New South W some years ago, Now my dear Sir I have given you all the
News of Family affairs and I Conclude with Saying how happy I will be to hear
from you on all occasions. I am getting quite sound in my health after four
years suffering,

I Remain My dear Cousin
Yours very truly
James H. Reibey

From Raville Farm

This recently discovered letter, 27th July, 1831, of Mary Reibey, written to a farmer on the Hawkesbury River from her farm, Raville Farm, has been offered to me anonymously by a Coogee friend. This short note, so far, is the first letter, signed by her to an Australian addressee, that I have come across. There are copies of other business transactions made by her; this note has her genuine signature. There was a dispute about temporary road access until the authorities made a public road. In another (copied) letter Mary Reibey advises her tenant to quietly allow access as long as the tenant farmer replaces the sliprails. N.I. August 1992.

Entally House – Hadspen, Tasmania
Built in 1820 by Thomas Haydock Reibey II
Son of Mary & Thomas Reibey
Now a National Trust property

1796– 1842
Thomas Haydock Reibey II — son of Mary Reibey
Builder of Entally – Tasmania
Oil in possession of his great grandson Oliver William-Powlett of Cadhay, Devon

Letter 19

From Thomas Haydock Reibey II, now in London to his Cousin David Hope from 3 Canterbury Villas, Edgeware Road, London. Sept.8th 1838.

For Thomas II is now in London , in a leased cottage which he now wants to quit. For he will at last arrange schooling for the boys.Tom III was now,1838 nearing 17 years and James was 15. What an uprooting for them, previously educated at he Longford School in Tasmania. Note,their sister is already married to Gov Arthur's nephew, and these two are also in England visiting his relatives in Plymouth.

Tom II has placed his boys at a London school but he is not satisfied. Like his Mother, Mary, he demannds the best as he conceives this expensive educational excursion. He organises a live-in situation where the boys Tutor receives them as members of that tutor's family, in Devonshire...very largely on the recommendation of the Arthur relatives. Terms are one hundred guineas each boy per Term .Later a Tutor went with the boys to Oxford to the Landowners' College. Tom II is happy.The whole family have travelled the long ten thousand sea miles, Richarda as well. Of interest is the visit of Mr Redfern, the expolitician surgeon of NSW.. Like travellers today Tom anxiously awaits letters from Australia, with news of his sick brother James, his mother Mary and the home news. The Hopes have dined with him in London. He speaks of advising one prospective migrant .O'Denny. There is an interesting letter from Mr Denny.

3 Canterbury Villas
Edgware Road
London Sept.8th.

My dear Sir

I must apologise for my long silence in not replying sooner to your very kind letter of the 18th. ultimo, but really my mind has been so ill at ease the last three weeks in consequence of my premature decision in placing my sons at a school in London, where I am sorry to find no probability of their making that improve ment I at first contemplated; the school being more adapted for very young boys, half their time is lost by not having the benefit of the society and conversation of the school master, who spends the whole of his evenings from home - I have therefore been compelled to determine upon sending them to Devonshire, at the end of this Quarter to be placed under the care and tuition of a Revd. Mr Barnes, who is, by my son (in-law) Mr Arthur and all his relations, spoken very highly of & who has a family of accomplished sisters. My sons are received as members of his family and his number is limited to to six, all highly respectable. I have been much pleased with a letter I received from him, his terms are one hundred and twenty guineas each, per annum, and have consequently arranged to send them off as near the first of October as possible. Mrs Reibey (Richarda) will accompany them to Plymouth, to join Mr & Mrs Arthur who feel great reluctance to part with their relations there - I am, unfortunately, hampered with a cottage which I engaged for 6 months but have written off to the proprietor who is now spending a short time at Harrogate, to request he will allow me to give it up at the end of the quarter, which I am in hopes he will do, and immediately I can rid myself of it I purpose paying you a visit to spend a short time before I join my family at Plymouth. I should have been glad could I have managed to have been with you by the 27th of this month, but that is impossible - Mr Redfern called about a fortnight after he had been in London. I was not at home, but called upon him the following day and for so short an acquaintance was much pleased with him. I invited him to dinner but he had made some engagement to visit Kent, having given up his original intention of going to the Continent, when you see his mother will you remember me very kindly-

I am in daily expectation of receiving accounts from Van Diemens Land which I am very anxious about, as I left my brother James in a very precarious state of health. I am also in hopes soon to hear from my mother, and sisters-

Your brother William & his wife, together with Mr.,Mrs. & Miss Atkinson dined with us on Wednesday last - Mrs Hope with her daughter Celia is now spending a few days with us - I am very anxious to see you and hope soon to have that pleasure, but in the mean time I would only say your letters are very acceptable. pray write often I pay postage for your letters with great delight - My sons have this moment stopped home, being half holiday, to dine with us, they beg, together with Mrs. Reibey to be very kindly remembered to you - Believe me

My dear Cousin, your's very sincerely- Thomas Reibey

P.S. If you should see Mr J 0 Denny say that I have not forgotten my promise and will in the course of a few days send him letters to Van Diemens Land, which I trust will be of service to him. I believe he does not sail till the first of the month.

1842 – 1892?
The City of Sydney, N.S.W., by John Skinner Prout
Watercolour, possibly on lithographed base

James Haydock Reibey II - grandson of Mary Reibey
Became Vicar of Denbury, Devon, untill he died
Oil painting in possession of his grandson, Oliver William-Powlett of Cadhay,
Devon

Letter 20

Letter 20 comm. January 11, 1843 /4 To Cousin David, Glasgow from Penciville, New Town near Sydney. written by Mary Helen Thompson, granddaughter of our Mary Reibey, she was just 22 years of age.. Eldest child of Eliza and Thomas Thomson, she together with her Mama and very sick father and one called Thomasina and her young sisters have some time past, been visiting Scotland. One suspects at Mary Reibey's instigation. Eliza had 9 children by 1844, the youngest, Thomas Thomson II, being a mere 4 years of age. .They have finally returned to Sydney after what appears to have been a six month voyage. I place this letter, for charm and information, next to Jane Penelope's delightful letter to her Cousin David, written some twenty years beforehand. It is rather wistful, with plenty of information about the family. The voyage has been difficult in as much as becalming was such controlling element in sail travel. They left Leith on monday 1st July and finally reached Melbourne (spoken of always as Town Port Phillip) on 12th December. Her description of the incidents on the voyage are fascinating; the passing vessels "speaking" each other by signals and possibly "trumpets" very much as Newton Fowell similarly described communication at sea way back in 1788. Helen, young spinster gives the male single passengers a serve, complaining very much and in detail of their lack of attention. Interestingly It is Mr & Mrs Wills who entertain the whole family at his Port Phillip home;

very nice place with a beautifull house upon it...

Then there are the snippets about the family members. Uncle Innes (Elizabeth's Lieut Innes) is back in Sydney, meeting the ship. Uncle James is dead, the last of Mary R's sons. Thomas Reibey II had died very suddenly in 1842. Strangely his boys did not know till they arrived back in NSW from Oxford. Grandma (Mary R). is in better health, in consequence of her new home in New Town. Mary Helen writes:

We are all staying with my Grandmama. it is about 3 miles from Sydney and a beautiful place it is/ every one says that it has been the saving of Grandmamma's health ... now she is well and so stout...

A sad account of the Colony's Depression reads very much as could be said of Australia, today, 1992.

bad as our state is we are very thankful that we are not as bad as many who once drove their carriage...who have been obliged to go into the Insolvent Court

As her father Thomas Thomson has been free to travel out of Australia one imagines that he was cleared of all debts. Yet they return to much trouble which the young lady guilessly relates. They are to live at Rosetta in North Tasmania and hope to lease small farms. Young Thomas Reibey III and James and their wives have visited Sydney on their return from Oxford, on the death of Thomas Reibey II..She speaks of James Reibey II's son Jimmy Clack Reibey-..father of Charlotte Reibey..William Powlett. He too died young, 22 years of age in 1870 in Devon. The gallant Lieut. Thomson of 1820 is now bedridden,sadly, but I like to think that the large family coped. Mary Helen's last words

he is more helpless and cannot assist himself in the slightest degree/ he has to be carried by two people and cannot even lift a spoon to his mouth... another deprivation is that he cannot read and it is so difficult to amuse him for he will have someone to read to him

I like this daughter, Mary Helen Thomson.

To David Hope
5 Wellington Place
    Glasgow

Recd. 9 July 1844
7.30 a.m.

Sydney Pencilville(?)
January 11th 1843

My dear Cousin

You will say that I have quite forgotten my promise of writing to you immediately we arrived at our destination / when I tell you that we have been there nearly three weeks / but really I have been so busy and so unsettled since our arrival that I have been unable to spare time to write but as I know you dislike apologies so I will make none but leave you to imagine that I have not been able to write before and now to proceed to particulars. We sailed as you know from Leith on Monday the 31st. of July we went on very well for two days and saw the Orkney islands though at a great distance but after we passed them the wind became foul and (?) so all day we were very close to the land - Cape Wrath - where we saw a great number of vessels at one time there were fifteen in sight we spoke one / She was from India bound to Sunderland. Our foul wind lasted till the 19th. of August when it changed but the fair wind only lasted one day when it again veered round and continued alternately a foul wind or a dead calm till the 1st of September when we got into the trades but those only lasted us for a few days at a time it was so often calm. Mamma wrote you by a vessel we spoke called the "Ca???" but I do not know if she said anything of the first part of the voyage. We saw several vessels before we spoke the Ca*???* but did not speak any we signalized one for some hours one day / it was very amusing to see the the vessel putting up and taking down signals as quick as possible - she was a Dutch East Indiaman from Rotterdam bound for Batavia she was a vessel of a thousand tons. We crossed the Line on the 27th. of September - it was very hot and <u>we</u> were becalmed near the line but after we had crossed it we proceeded very well and had a splendid passage to the Cape of Good Hope. Captain Morrison said that he never had such a fine passage from the line to the Cape as he had this time. Part of the time we had what we called rather rough weather - we were under three reefed topsails several times and a slight gale of wind but we ought really to esteem ourselves fortunate never to have been round the world and to have had one heavy gale of wind. We arrived at Port Phillip on the 2nd. of December where we remained a week and a very pleasent week it was for we stayed at Mr Wills's the whole time / he insisted upon the whole of us going out to his place to remain there all the time the ship stayed / both him and Mrs. Wills were very very kind to us they seemed as if they could not do enough for us and are very anxious that some of us should go and spend some time with them at Port Phillip, they have got a very nice place with a beautiful house upon it. We sailed from Wills and Town Port Phillip on the 12th. of December but from contrary winds could not get outside the heads for a whole week but lay at anchor inside the Head from Tuesday Morning to the following Monday / we were a week on our passage - having had only three days fair wind the whole way. We arrived on the 25th Christmas day it was late in the afternoon before we (?) and in consequence of having powder on board we could not go up to the Wharf but had to anchor some distance down the harbour / my Uncle Innes was in waiting with a boat long before we anchored but owing to Papa's state of health and the lateness of the evening neither Thomasina or him went on shore but myself accompanied by my sisters at least some of them went on shore to my *(?) (?) (?)* / we found my dear Grandmamma who I am happy to say is in better health than she has been for years. I suppose long ere this you will have heard of the death of poor Uncle James who died on the 11th. of September / he had been suffering more than usual the attacks of gout had been more severe and more frequent and he had called in more advice the first day the new doctor saw him he had asked what should be his diet the two Doctors turned round to consult and when they looked at him again he was dead; though long ill *(?)* the manner of his death was very sudden / but death is always sudden come when at *(?)* it never enters a family singly but cuts off two or three ere it ceases / poor Grandmamma has now lost all her sons and two of them within the twelve months. We heard of Uncle James's death when we arrived at Port Phillip from a perfect stranger who told Thomasina not knowing that she was any relation to Mr James Reibey. We are all staying with my Grandmamma it is about three miles from Sydney and a beautiful place it is / every one says that it has been the saving of Grandmamma's health for before she came out here she was in very bad health and now she is very well and so stout*(?)* and is never troubled with her health at all / I can assure you it was a very agreeable surprise to find her in so much better health for when we left ill in bed and subject to constant attacks of asthsma.

You will be surprised to hear that we are going to Launceston to be at Rosetta as we found our affairs in a much worse state than we had any idea of / they have not got one penny of rent from Rosetta but have brought us into debt for ejecting the last tenant; the bank of Australia has failed and we have lost the thousand pounds that the Youngs placed there for us to get the interest / so we have literally nothing of our own to depend upon for if we let Rosetta it is not likely that we should get any rent no one *(?)* now a day we have nothing to go a farthing with and if we had it would be no use for nothing can be sold meat is a penny a pound sheep can be bought a shilling a head / cows five shillings and all the settlers are not attempting to sell anything but are actually boiling down all their sheep and cattle for fat for export so you may fancy what a dreadful state the country is in / we are therefore going to live in the house at Rosetta and are going to try and let the farm out in small pieces to try if we can get some little rent there, my brother is very anxious we should go down there he thinks it will be the best thing we can do / I suppose we shall leave Sydney in about three weeks or a month I wonder when our travelling days will be over I am sure we are all weary of this wandering.

Thomasina desires me to say that she is really so harassed and so completely out of spirit that she really has not the heart to sit down and write but she will write you a long letter shortly / she is not very well though a great deal better than when we left Scotland for she has entirely lost the dreadful cough she had when you last saw her but she is so out of spirits with the deplorable situation of our affairs that she looks quite ill / but bad as our state is we are very thankful that we are not as bad as many are who once drove their carriage and are now so reduced that they can hardly get their daily bread / oh it is dreadful the state of misery the country is in there is hardly one who have not been obliged to go into the Insolvent court / there is a talk than the times have begun to improve but every one says they should see it. I am sure I hope it would soon take a favourable turn for our own sakes and that of all belonging to us for all of our relations are suffering like ourselves.

Papa is much the same as when we left that is in health but he is more helpless and cannot assist himself in the slightest degree he has to be carried by two people and cannot even lift a spoon to his mouth but has to be fed like a child / another deprivation is that he cannot read and it is so difficult to amuse him for he will have some one to read to him.

Young Thomas Reibey was here some little time before we arrived / all here are just delighted with both him and his wife they remained about three weeks in Sydney / when he arrived here he had not heard of his father's death - poor fellow he was much shocked; have you heard <u>anything</u> of young James Reibey no one here has heard anything of or from him for this long time and they cannot imagine what has become of him. Will you make some enquiries about him. What do you think of the young men (gentlemen I cannot call them) on board the Midlothian never adressing a word to one of the ladies during the whole voyage and not only that but took every opportunity during the whole voyage of insulting us most openly and grossly even at the cuddy table. They used to call us fools use to carricature me and of and at us in the most disgusting manner / one of them a Mr Young from Edinburgh wrote two letters to Mamma copies of which she means to send to you as a specimin you never in your life heard or saw anything like the disgraceful conduct of people who called themselves gentlemen but to which name none of them had or ever will have pretensions to behave in so shameful a manner to a (?) of young and unprotected girls for none of us having a brother and knowing Papa was in that state of health that he could take no notice of their conduct / two of them in a more disgraceful manner than I can tell you Mamma will write you all about it as(?) it often made our blood boil to hear the disgusting remarks that were made at us at the dinner table / the Doctor to whom you introduced us on board the steamer never took wine with us the whole of the voyage / he used to talk to Papa of us of course knowing well that so young a child would tell us anything and everything that was said and used to sit at the dinner table (when I had the honour of sitting next to him) and turn his back to me and take out a book and read he used to join and approve of all the others conduct / far more could I tell you if I had only the time and patience of their cowardly conduct such as bowing to us and kissing their hand to us at the time when they never spoke to us; one thing was that we did not care for their acquaintance but were so happy and independent amongst us and I know this very independence (?) them for they saw us so very happy and caring so little whether they spoke to us or not; the only one who behaved well and he did behave well was the first mate he is a <u>Glasgow</u> man and really he did behave well and politely what none of the rest did / of course the Captain behaved well to us /

The first mate's name is Mr. Robertson and if you meet him in Glasgow pray thank him in our name for his kindness and attention to us during the voyage / we should have fared very badly if it had not been for him and the captain - And now I will say a few words about our Glasgow friends I hope Mrs. Dickson and all her family are well / We heard that Mrs ?ra?son was getting on pretty well but we did not see her. How is Mr. Fergusson getting on I have no doubt *(?)* that he will get on well for he is a very good and a very gentlemanly young man / I am sure he would not have behaved the way the *(?)* did if he had been on board the Midlothian / give our kind respects to him and say we often talk and think of him. How are Mr. & Mrs. *(?)* give our kind regards to them and all enquiring Glasgow friends we shall always retain a grateful *(?)* of our visit to Glasgow and the kindness we received there. All my sisters are quite well and desire their best and kindest love to you / they will write you in a short time but you know they are not good pen correspondents*(?)* Grandmamma is writing to you I believe but when she means to finish the letter I do not know / she desires her kind love to you. My Aunt Innes whom you used to quiz me for talking so much about is quite well and desires her kind regards to you. I do not think I have any news to tell you but hope you will excuse this uninteresting letter but I really do not know of anything that will amuse you so for from Scotland for you like nothing out of Glasgow though you did make much of your foreign cousins.

When you write to Penelope tell her that I will write to her very soon give my kindest love to her in which all my sisters most cordially join. It is very hot weather here but I do not like it half so well as the fine snowy weather of Scotland.

I do not think you like a crossed letter but you will like it better at any rate than a double letter for postage is very high

And now I think I will conclude as you think I daresay it is high time and with kind love from Mamma and all my sisters in which believe me I most sincerely join

I remain

my dear Cousin

Your very sincerely attached
friend and cousin

Mary Helen Thomson

Letter 21

*F*rom Mary Reibey of Pencilville, New Town near Sydney to David Hope, dated 21st June 1845.

This is of course, a special letter for the reader-researcher. It is the last extant letter from Mary Reibey, as in 1992. Tying up the information already extracted from the preceeding letters, with hindsight we can feel the gradual acceptance of lonely old age, although the family all seem to rally around. We know that Grandsons John Atkinson and James Thomson are to leave their banking employment and will be working together on her Shoalhaven Property, NSW. Eventually John sold his half to James, whose descendants still cherish and till the Shoalhaven soil. At first Mary complains bitterly of Lieut. Thomson's failure to repay her, or so it reads. She rails at the bitter deaths of all her sons, but then explores her faith in her God. Old age and its loneliness upsets her as all old people are upset by this inevitable fact of life. Yet the letter explains to her dear Cousin how much delight she has in this new venture, setting up an estate in New Town. She is 68 years and she lived another six years...The New Town Estate is 21 acres in extent; she can see the sand hills at Botany Bay. A new house is being built alongside for widowed Eliza Thomson and her children. She tells of the great joy of listening to grandson Archdeacon Tomson Reibey preach in nearby St Peters church. The Hopes and Reibeys exchange the Sydney Herald and the Blackburn newspaper. Mary left behind a great family clan.

I send you a Sydney
Herald date 20 June /45

Pencilville
New Town

Near Sydney
21st. June /45

My dear Cousin

It is so long since I have heard from you and which I intirely blame myself for as of late I have become a very bad correspondent not only with you but with every one/ for with my breavements and embarrasments I almost gave up every enjoyment and social comfort till when I came to reflect I thought it wicked and sinful to dispair / it is the Lords will and it is right we should be punished or we should not know ourselves, / you may remember in my last I told you of my making myself responsible for a certain persons bills to a very large amount/ will you believe it I have never had the slightest help towards returning them altho promised and I am sure might have been dupe(?), but while they know my property is the fountain,/ I am obliged to pay to the last pound to meet them & as the Bank are very kind in giving me time I shall best enabled to get through it in two or 3 years to save my property for my children/ and which I am obliged to exercise the greatest prudence and ecconomy still in my old age and so many years of perseverance and industry it is hard to be deprived of the many comforts I have been acccustomed too/ but that I do not think so much of as the unprincipled feeling towards me in the matter/ so long as I can be punctual in my payments and do what is right in the sight of the Lord I am willing to give up all enjoyment in this world trusting in the mercifull goodness of an all seeing God / I am afraid I shall tire you with my complaints but my dear Cousin I know you are nearly all I have to simphathise with me and I have ever since I knew you considered you more as a Br. than a Cousin / I open my mind to you more than any one else since the Melancholly death of all my sons - my soninlaw Mr Atkinson is living at Van Deimans Land or he would be of great assistance to me as far as advice etc: he is an exellent man a good husband good Father and a sincere friend and if we may judge by all accounts we hear *(?)* the Character of a honest and just man / he is a Magistrate at Launceston / dont you think that I ought to be proud of all my family turning out so respectable all my sons and soninlaws with the exception of Mr Thomson were Magistrates.

Mrs Atkinson and family 7 in number are coming up in a few days to pay me a visit several of them being in ill health which I hope the change may do them good/ Mr Atkinson will come up himself in a few months to take them back and me also as he says/ but I am now so taken up with my residence that I told you I had purchased I do not like to move and notwithstanding my dear purchase as I told you befor I consider it was the best I ever made as it has quite renovated my health/ and I am now in the enjoyment of as good health as ever I was, excepting my age and it is to the salubrous air that I account it to,/ it is a beautiful spot we have a pleasent view of the Botany Bay Heads and the sea and I am making a great improvement on it\ there is 21 acres of all pretty good land I have an exellent garden on it which I re-made myself / it was all bush and trees when I purchased it with the exception of a small patch round about the House / I now also Fenced it all in with a close pailing; Since I have laid out a great deal of money on it since I bought it/ I also intend to Build a nice Cottage on it (as soon as I can recover myself a little) for Mrs Thomson and her family were she will be free from House rent a good garden and many advantages / poor girl she is now living in Launceston, were her Farm is but it being let before she arrived there she was obliged to rent a Cottage and it is so expensive voyaging backwards and forwards l she must stay their till I get her House to live in here / do you hear of any of the young if they are inclined to assist her it is a hard task for her with 8 Children only one able to do anything/ that is her son James a very good youth he is and I think clever / he is in the Bank of Australasia at Launceston and I think his salary is £180 per annum/ but they are kept very close to it almost to the (?) of their health indeed young John Atkinson was obliged to leave on account of his bad health being impaired by too close attention,/ he was in the Branch Union Bank I think he got £100 per annum / forgot to tell you that Mrs Atkinson would have been with me before but she lost one of her litle girls / she died very suddenly and a great favourite she was with them/ she was called Celia Alice after my lamented dear girl/ they both took it very bad indeed / you see in so short a time so many deaths in one family ought to learn us to prepare for the one thing needful/ Mrs Innes is expecting to have an addition to her family next month will make seven / she has now 3 boys and 3 girls and I am glad to say she is looking as well and young as her eldest Daughter which is 15.years of age/ they are all very fine Children her Eldest Bessey is two inches taller than her mama and she is that much taller than poor Celia was/ they desire to be kindly remembered to you I think I have given you an acct of the most part of my female branch / I must now tell you that I had the pleasure of my two Grandsons and their wives they both coming by the way of Sydney I had not seen them since they were boys before they as you know are two very fine young men/ Thomas was ordained some time back at V. Deimans Land / he his mother and wife was up with us lately he preached in the parish Church of St Peters were I go / when I heard him my feelings was so overcome that I cannot discribe to you/ he made a very short visit on acct of his affairs requiring him / I believe he-would sooner reside here than in V.D.Land for that place is getting into an awful state through the great influx of Convicts being sent their/ I must revert to your own family in the first place may I ask if you have Changed your situation - I began to think so through not hearing from you and let me know how poor John gets on/ their is no person on this earth has a more sincere regard for his welfare than I have altho he has not written me / I do not think it is but of any ill feeling to me but want of thought/ give him and Mrs H. my most grateful thanks and remembrance for their attentions to me & my family when in Manchester/ I shall never forget the (?) hour of my life / also to William and his amiable wife make my kind regards to them not forgetting Alice and her spouse & her son,/ I recd 3 Blackburn papers the other day which I thank you for they afford me a great deal of Gratification to hear anything of my own Town, I sent you one Sydney Herald with the (?) of the Bank of Australia & Australasia & thought it would be Interesting to you / have you heard anything of Mr Cobal(?) lately you may thank him for me for the two *(?)* he so kindly sent me by Mrs Thomson/ but it must have been quite a mistake on his part he could not have known me. I must now Conclude with my most affectionate regards from

your ever Cousin M. Reibey

Mrs Foster is still living with me and is something better tempered than usual

Extra Information on Building Activities of Mary Reibey.

From Notes made by The Architect Verge, ed. by his grandson, W. J. Verge, 1962, pps 197–199.

This is a rare book, not available.

In 1803, grant given at Lot 70 (near Macquarie Place) to build a house 50 ft by 16 ft., to be of two stories of stone. Finally built by 1809. Occupied till lease to Bank of NSW for £160 per annum. There was a dispute about the repairs to this house in 1834 of some £21.

Cottage was built in 1826 on the present site of the GPO. Extensive. Land was 100 ft to the East of the Tank Stream.

1833– 1834 M. Reibey built shops and a dwelling in lower George Street. In 1867 an old Reibey cottage in George Street was destroyed by fire.

1848 an engraving showed an unbroken row of houses in Baderham (sic) included 4 elegant shops and a row of houses.

In her letters Mary Reibey calls her house Penciville, New Town. Verge notes it as Reibey House of Station Street, Newtown.

Nance Irvine, September 1992.

Letter 22

ELIZABETH INNES, Mary's youngest daughter, had eight children the second being Celia married to Army man Pym. Letter 22 is from Chatham Barracks, London, dated March 14th, 1852. She has endured a long six months on board a slow sailing vessel while her husband has been whisked off with his regiment in a Man of War. She is not one to be stirred by exotic eastern ports. Spouse is studying for an exam to elevate him to an Adjutancy. London is frightening in its intensity after Australia, ie in 1852. She writes

the prices of things astonish me, everything so much higher than in Sydney

But then Celia admits that the gold rush has inflated prices of goods and services in Sydney. We hear a granddaughter's opinion of what is happening to Grandma (Mary R.). Otherwise this is our final bird's eye view of the Sydney Clan.

N.M.Barracks Chatham
March 14th/52

My dear Mr Hope

I received your kind letter a short time since and as you said it would give you great pleasure to hear from me sometime I now intend answering it. Although I fear cannot write a very interesting letter from this place, it is very dull and the same things happen day after day but I must try my best, you tell me to give you an account of my voyage it was a very long and tedious one we had little bad weather, but so many calms and the ship was such a very slow sailer, we left Sydney on the twenty fourth of August and did not arrive in England until the eleventh of January very nearly five months, I should not have thought it half as long if my husband had been with me but he was obliged to come home in the Man of War he went out in. I suffered very much from sea sickness and feel quite a dread of the sea now but I think I should soon summon courage enough to go out to Sydney again, it seemed so strange to me to be away from all my friends, We were obliged to put in at Pernambuco for provisions such a wretched place it is, we only stayed two days there but it was quite enough, the heat was so intense we could hardly bear to walk across the sheds(?), I hope it will be my last visit there, it is a fearfully dirty place, but perhaps I am telling you what you know already, for I daresay you have been there - You want to know how I like England, it is hardly fair of me to judge for I have seen very little of it, I have been to London several times but was glad to leave it, I was quite bewildered and must confess astonished with everything / it is certainly a wonderful place I have not seen any sights yet but hope soon to be able to spend a few hours in that way, Mr Pym is very busy just now studying for an examination for a Staff appointment - he is very anxious to get an Adjutancy but I am sorry to say has not very much interest I he however intends to try what he can do for himself/ if he succeeds it will make us very comfortable, for England is an expensive place to live in, the prices of things astonish me, every thing so much higher than in Sydney, at least when I left, but most likely there has been a great change on account of the Gold Mines, such numbers of people from all quarters of the world are flocking there attracted with the accounts of the quantity of gold there is to be found. I suppose you have had an account of the piece weighing a hundred pounds that was found in one solid lump but the person who purchased it to send home very foolishly broke it up it would have been much better to send it as it was for people are inclined to doubt the fact, but it is quite fun I can assure you. The people are mad about going to the Diggings, Sydney I fear for some time will be in a sad state, all the servants and labouring men were leaving and wages enormously high, The man left Grandmama because she would not give him more than a pound a week besides keeping him rather absurd is it not! I have not heard From Sydney since I wrote to you but am expecting long letters every day, I hope if you have a spare moment you will write to her soon, I am much obliged for your offer of showing me all the wonders of your beautiful country but I am afraid it will be a long time before I can have that pleasure / I should indeed like to see Scotland, must live in hopes of doing so, some day before I go out again. I have your parcel still, it is quite safe, if I have an opportunity of sending it to your brother at Deptford I shall be sure not to forget it. You will be tired reading such a long uninteresting letter but I told you at first that there was no news of any interest in this place to tell you, We have been very fortunate in getting nice quarters in Barracks and I dare say in course of time I shall like the place very well but we are both anxious to go out again/ Mr Pym says if he does not succeed in getting a

Staff appointment, he will try and go in the ship that relieves the Man of War now there,/ I cannot tell you how anxious I am to see my dear Mother and all my friends once again,/ Grandmama often talks of coming to England but I do not think she ever will, indeed at her time of life it would be very foolish to risk such a long voyage, She has a very pretty place a few miles out of town / until the last few months has enjoyed excellent health, I forget if I told you that both my Aunts Atkinson and Thomson were in Sydney when I last heard/ they went up to see Grandmama, the latter only intended staying a very short time I should think she was quite tired of moving about so much, they have left Melborne and gone back to their old house in Launceston, / I cannot tell you much of the Arthurs or Reibeys We never hear from them but I believe they are all getting on very well, of course you know James has a little son, he is now about three years old, his wife has been very dangerously ill lately, Mary has an immense family of little ones, I think there are nine of them, altogether and all very nice children, one is very delicate, indeed I fear she will not live, she is subject to dreadful fits perhaps she may grow out of them some of the doctors say she will / I think I must now say good bye Mr Pym sends with me our kindest regards and

Believe me dear Mr Hope

Your sincere Cousin

Celia L. Pym

1821 – 1912
Thomas Haydock Reibey III — Tasmania
Grandson of Mary Reibey
one time Premier of Tasmania and M.H.A. for thirty years

1871 – 1954
Mrs. Emily Charlotte William-Powlett née Reibey
Great granddaughter of Mary Reibey Granddaughter of Rev. James Haydock Reibey
In possession of Oliver William-Powlett, Devon
Her son – Peverill – became an Admiral as well as serving a period as
Governor of Rhodesia

Letters 23/24/25

The Reibey Letters conclude with Grandson, Tom Reibey III's last three Letters from Entally, Tasmania. Written to his beloved niece Charlotte, (Lotte and Sugar Plum to her family). She became Mrs Barton Wallop William-Powlett, dying in 1954 Tom was sturdy like his Grandmother, Mary. I think of him as the Venerable Philanderer, Squire Reibey of Entally.

Tom III- ruthless, charming... this is his tale. Entally, his state, was the country estate which mirrored England at this other end of the world in Van Diemens Land striving to be Tasmania in the 19th century. He lived to become Premier of the state.

There was the court drama which was reported in toto in all Mainland and Tasmanian newspapers . Many more details came... from the Diary of his nephew. Rev Charles Arthur . Surprisingly much was extracted from a court drama;more than is reported by today's hungry tabloids. The infamous Reibey libel case reflects the ambivalent morals of those conservative years of the 1870s. It concerned his alleged approaches to his 30 year old goddaughter. Tom was 49 years old when he challenged Harry, the libelling and allegedly injured husband of Goddaughter Blomfield. Anecdotal reports about this legal tangle throughout the seventy odd years of Reibey's adult life have become part of the great legends of Tasmania. He did lose the case, paid up £2000, shed his Archdeaconry but remained with the church. Tom was important to his District.

Without him ?

Well without him there would not have been the sumptuous entertaining of the Vice Regal parties who happily transferred from Hobart to Entally to Tom's beautifully maintained cricket pitch, his shooting matches and hunting meets, not to mention his stimulating company. For Thomas Reibey was an Oxford man,of Trinity, the land owners' College... As was the Tasmanian Governor Du Cane from Exeter College. Without Archdeacon Reibey there would never have occurred such a bizarre libel case, no cause célèbre to titillate the Tasmanians. Their Victorian decorum at risk! For he was a man who invited envy.The most popular and sought after Entally House celebration was the annual cricket extravaganza of New Year. He remained king in his Entally castle till his death in 1912, and was a member of the Tasmanian House of Assembly for some 30 years.

During the seventies the newspapers were often full of criticism. The smug puritans crucified him in letters to the Editors. Editors who I guess, as ever, were looking for the easy dollar. There was much jealousy afoot among the less blessed clergy. For Tom was a very weathy man, the Grandson of the legendary matriarch, Mary Reibey.

At the foot of Mary Reibey's rainbow, was a hoard of carefully acquired wealth..mercantile interests,maritime activities and land, land land . It reached from the Hawkesbury River to the South Coast of NSW including a stunning estate of 60 acres in the New Town City of Sydney .Eventually there she died in 1855. She wrote

(Letter 21) of the joys of her new Town house while viewing the sand hills of Botany Bay. In this year of 1992 those hills can still be glimpsed from Newtown. Astutely looking to the future of this new country, Mary had settled two grandsons on the lush South Coast farmlands of New South Wales. .The twentieth century Thomson family is still grazing cattle there. . In Tasmania she had watched the increasingly prosperous Entally Estate arise on rolling northern river flats. Arisen on a land grant of 2000 acres on which the matriarch had sworn by affidavit she meant to settle herself. Well her sons did.

I doubt if the children (Letter 7) let alone the grandchildren actually knew of Mary's convict status in the late eighteenth century. It was convenient to forget. For emancipist she certainly was. Ironically descendants today (and there are many, amongst them the great great grandson Oliver William-Powlett, 1991 high sheriff in Devon) revel in the record of this grand little lady, of early Australia.

Tom Reibey confounded his enemies and delighted the friends of his electorate. For from July 1876 to August 1903 he held the House of Assembly seat for Westbury, nearly 30 long years!

Entally House was his kingdom.

He lovingly created the kennels of beagles and pedigreed settlers. Legend, rumour, in which I guess there is a modicum of truth, proclaimed that the beagles "came from Lord Lewis' celebrated pack, from England of course. The setters came from the Prince Consort's kennels. Allegedly it was tactfully stated the breeders were sent out by a 'friend'."

His greatest joy, so 'tis said, was the breeding of thoroughbreds. The "best horse I ever owned" was Stockwell, disputed winner of the Melbourne Cup in 1882. Then there was Malua which won the Yan Yean Stakes. Malua was a bay stallion with a reputation akin to the later Pharlap. Malua was said to be the greatest all-rounder ever to be bred in Australia. There were 90 horses raced from Entally stables. After all it was terrific, in our modern sense of that word, that Reibey's crew could cross the turbulent Tasman and defeat the local Melbourne fanciers. Tom insisted that he never laid a bet. Moreover, in various interviews given later in his life, he repeatedly maintained

They were true and fair sportsmen in those days - no humbug, no pulling and everyone out to win. There was no chance of asking any of those man to 'pull' a horse!

It's also claimed that the Squire of Entally never lodged a protest. He had a string of winners in the Oakleigh Plate, V.R.C. Newmarket and V.R.C. Grand National Hurdle Race. Later Malua did win the 1884 Melbourne Cup. Not surprising that Tom had a lot to do with the financing and development of the Carrick Race course. His riders always wore silk of old rose colour. That appeals to me. It reminds me of the little loyal Kate Reibey. Always in the background but always there in support. She waved off the pack of hounds with the Hunt when they left Entally to chase the deer. One journal insisted that the deer always outsmarted the hounds. It was released to well known haunts complete with a pink bow. The bow to warn men that this stag was a pet and special. The hype read;

Very cunning and knowing full well what was expected of him the deer would make off at full speed over logs, ditches and fences leaving a good scent for the hounds which despite their most desperate efforts never caught up with him. A good feed of steamed bran and oats would welcome the stag back to his home in the shed behind the stables. Here he would enjoy himself in safety behind barred doors where the panting hounds would come at last and rave round the walls to get in at him.

Well you must agree it's a comforting story for the Quorn Hunt to have believed.

Another journalist wrote;

Thomas Reibey was well known as a breeder and owner who did not believe in training horses to a shadow, they were commonly thought to carry too much condition. He kept and and ran horses for the pure love of sport and it was his proud boast that he had never made a wager.

Entally was maintained as a show place. The famous Cricket pitch was always beautifully prepared. This certified by an old gardener, Mr. Glenn who together with a nurseryman, a Mr. Thorpe cared for the grounds for over 30 years. The stories are the same from wherever in the realm of journalism. I imagine the tall Tom Reibey led by his handsome, very long white beard, strolling within his demesne savouring the twilight of his successful long life. I have never found a reference to a Blomfield in any of the newspaper cuttings, nor of the press at that time. I guess the libel case can scarcely be compared to a Whitlam... Fraser/Kerr affair, but certainly at the time of 1870 it was a mind blowing publicity not entirely favourable to the Venerable Philanderer.
So what of his last years?
Little Kate, Catherine Reibey died on July 14, 1896. They were together for 52 long years. From this whole story she shines, if in a lesser role than the Venerable. She shines because nowhere can I find any fuss, any complaint about her rather dull life. Dull after her butterfly existence back in Tom's Oxford days. She behaved perfectly during the abortive libel case way back in 1870. Old photographs show her sitting upright in the buggy alongside the Honourable member. Catherine Reibey was buried in the graveyard of the unfinished little old church at Hadspen. One cause for me of disquiet is the fact that Tom 3rd could leave that church unfinished over so many years. (IN FACT IT

WAS NOT COMPLETED TILL THE 1950s) Yet he did leave it so. Eventually was buried there himself and with great honour being paid.

From letters found in Devon in that wonderful old manor house, Cadhay, Ottry St Mary, not to mention the helpful old Bible sitting on a bookshelf in their long Gallery, I've been able to piece together Tom 3rd's close ties with his brother's family. I talk of James Haydock Reibey 2nd, vicar of Denbury, Devon.

The reverend James' son, Jimmy, that is James Clack Reibey had a delightful childhood and youth. He enjoyed the best that could be offered to an English county boy. A scholar of Eaton College, with visits away to Scotland and the west coast with gentry companions. These letters of Jimmy are most entertaining but really have no place in this tale. Save to point out the amazing extent and success of exconvict Mary Reibey's ambitions for her extended family. Her boys and then her grandsons travelled to the mother country and to the best schools to establish their future connections when and if they returned to the Colony. Moreover the boys attended Oxford together with a tutor.

The letters of young Jimmy Reibey are a source of much information of those years, of joy. He came down and married one Emily. Within a year he was dead with some incurable glandular trouble. Letters to Entally had told of the trouble and the subsequent sad death of the young father to be. Yes Emily was pregnant. Her little girl Charlotte Reibey (Later known affectionately by today's families as Sugar Plum) was reared in the comfortable Victorian rectory at Denbury. Her letters are a further picture. Her Reibey Grandparents gave her everything that a county upper class young lady should enjoy. She tells of her balls in the London season and many charming happenings in the Devon district. She wrote constantly to Uncle Tom and Aunt Kate in Tasmania. She inherited Tasmanian property near Launceston through the first James Haydock Reibey, her great uncle. Since he and his wife Rebecca had no issue, all their accumulated wealth went to their English niece. Lotte Reibey (always pronounced Raby - maybe) married Barton Wallop William Powlett and came to live in Cadhay. With her husband, she visited Sydney and Launceston and became the light of Tom Reibey the III, her great uncle's later life as his letters show. The glorious portrait of Lotte William-Powlett, shows just how charming Mary Reibey's great great granddaughter was. All Mary's girls and their descendants appear to be lovely women in their portraits.

A vulnerable widower even at his age. Tom figures in the dreams, the imagination of some of those forgotten treasures, the spinsters of the District". Vide his letter to Lotte. I remembered that his brother James had (1890-) married his housekeeper, a woman with a teeny waist, very smart dresser, lace on her cuffs and her collar and muff, a bit over dressed really.

Here are the three last letters of Tom Reibey 3rd, which I have found at Cadhay.

1896
Entally 5 March.

My Dear Wallop and Lottie,

Ever since you drove away yesterday you have been hardly our of my mind and it was a grief to say "Goodbye". & when I saw Harrie with her companions meet you & cheer as you passed the gate I had to swallow a lump. Your visit has been very pleasant & grateful to us. We miss you! I don't like to look at your room as I pass. I can hardly believe that you have been with us & gone. It's all so like a dream! Bless you both - I hope you had a quiet passage over last night (TO MELBOURNE). It was very peaceful here, hardly any wind. What is your address in Sydney? Harrie & I hope to meet you on the 16th... I can't write any more. the house is dull. but we all miss you & wish you back with our very fond love to you both.

I am affectionately yours

Tho. Reibey.

Lottie and Barton had made a long honeymoon voyage to Entally from distant Devon.

Entally 27 April 1898

My Dear old Lottie

A few days ago the good news of your second child's birth & "both very well" was grateful to my heart & this night's mail has brought me a very pleasant photo of Newton. Many thanks for thinking of me. I am very thankful that your trouble is so well over & that you can rejoice that another man is born into the world. How many inches has Barton grown since the event Of course I am glad to be one of the Godfathers & hope some day to show that I am. The photo of Newton (FATHER OF THE PRESENT OWNER OF CADHAY) is now in the dining room... and I love to look at the dear child's face. Why? Because his eyes & face take me back to the past. I wish you were here today and could look at the oil portraits of my Father (TOMMY REIBEY 2nd) & your grandfather (JAMES REIBEY 2nd) in my library you would see that Newton is a Reibey.

The eyes are my dear fathers, Newton's great great grandfather and of my dear brother, his great grandfather. In the face of Newton I can see my Father & my brother. If in character, all that is generous & true, he proves to be like either, you & Barton will have cause to thankful & no cause to hang down your heads in shame. God grant that your boy may be like them both. I must compliment you on the way you dress Newton It is very charming. His hat is perfect. His legs and gaiters perfection. Of course you placed him in his chair while sitting for his photo... the knowing look of importance the little man assumes. Lottie dear, don't spoil him... On Monday next I must go to Hobart as Parliament opens on Tuesday. Mary & Harrie talk of going to Melbourne for the winter. & to be near Charlotte After a very long drought such as we have never known, rain has come again & the grass is getting green. A great relief to us... I fear the winter will be very severe for all stock after so much drought. The gossips are always ready in giving me another wife. Every single woman & every widow visiting Entally is to be the future Mrs Tom Reibey. So I have announced that I am engaged to Mrs Delaroyde a widow. Several are very curious to know who she is but I won't satisfy their curiosity but I will tell you as you will remember her. It is the lady who sells "Happles" at Perth station. She is almost 77 years old - a Roman Catholic... very stout weighs about 13 stone.

Kate Nelson wrote to Mary by the last mail and we were glad to hear that she and her daughter are well & enjoying life I have no more to tell you with this mail. So with love to you & Barton & your two sons I am your loving uncle

Tho. Reibey.

God Bless you Dear Lottie.

LOTTIE & BARTON BRED FOUR SONS: NEWTON, OLIVER, PEVERIL AND PETER. PEVERIL BECAME A GOVERNOR OF RHODESIA AND AN ADMIRAL OF THE FLEET, AS DID NEWTON. ALL FINE MEN. NEWTON'S SON, OLIVER IS AT THIS TIME HIGH SHERIFF OF DEVON.

Entally, 10th Oct 1901

My Dear old Lottie,

Had I been well I would have written sooner in reply to your letter of May 16th. I have had a very long & severe attack of Influenza & bronchitis. Though getting over it I am still weak & "sorry":. For the last fortnight I have rested, the train journey & night work in Parliament being too much for me.

(TOM REIBEY 3rd IS IN HIS EIGHTIETH YEAR) On wednesday last I attended the Longford Show & two of my horses, Sentry, a three year old & Mystic a lovely two year old were much admired and received the first prize for each. The long day - a most lovely Spring day, took a lot out of me. It was a successful Show in every department about 6000 present. And Tom has received Cudos (sic) & deserves it for his able management as Secretary. I am expecting him & Louisa here today, George his wife & Edith were here last night. I thought looking very bright. George & many more seem to me to have gone mad on Golf & perhaps in mining - the latter a very dangerous game. It always has been & ever will be... a few grow rich. Many, the majority prove very lean. Mary & Harrie are very well & take much interest in the flowers, cocks & hens etc etc of Entally. Just now the garden, trees & fields of Entally are coming into their new fresh summer beauty & the cherry trees abound in blossom. My new gardener has the place in perfect order, greenhouse full of flowers, hot house with ferns & grape vines giving promise of a bountiful yield of fruit. Last year we had fine grapes every morning for many weeks. Fishermen are out daily catching trout in the S. Esk & Meander & yesterday a party from L'eston *(LAUNCESTON)* had a picnic at the bridge. We are all excited at the Federal Tariff & I shall not be surprised if the Barton Ministry is defeated on it. Barton is not a Statesman. A politician pure & simple. The best man in his team, I think, is Sir George Turner. The Labour Party, beguiled by their selfish leaders, is increasing in power, and in all the States we have cause to fear, making troubles for years to come, under democratic leaders, men with nothing to lose. Socialism and even anarchy stare us in the face & as no statemen are here in Australia, Stump orators and demagogues have a terrible influence over the unthinking ignorant. It is that man Gladstone we have to thank for the evils growing fast, not only in Australia but in England, which threaten the destruction of property but of

liberty & even life/. Every tinker who can shout is now a power & the democratic parties a curse.

4.30 p.m.

Tom & Louisa have just left. Mary & Harry have gone out for a walk. I am too tired to do more than finish this letter. Don't be surprised if some day I walk into your house & ask for a night's lodging. For if I can arrange it I will try & come home next year in the hope of a sea voyage giving me new life. To see you again & your dear boys will be a real pleasure. I need rest & perfect change. All I have loved my Mother *(RICHARDA REIBEY NEE ALLEN)* Sister *(MARY ELLEN ARTHUR NEE REIBEY)* & Brother *(REVEREND JAMES HEYDOCK REIBEY, FATHER OF LOTTE)* & my wife *(CATHERINE MACDONNAL REIBEY NEE KYLE)* have left me. Earth is not the same to me & the lack of anything like honesty, gratitude or confidence in the society of the present day makes me positively yearn for rest somewhere.

With my love, dear Lottie, to you, husband & boys I am your affectionate uncle

Tho. Reibey.

I complete his story, probably absurdly but deeply hurt. I am bereft of a friend, Tom Reibey 3rd; boisterous no doubt, but a sensitive, intelligent loving man. He retired from politics in 1903, fully possessed of all his keen faculties till his death, Saturday 10th February, 1912, marked the end of an interesting life. The Squire of Entally, MHA Tasmania, received a grand ovation in death, from the newspapers in long columns; and from all the people of the district.

Tom would have liked that.

So would have his grandmother.

Nance Irvine. Sydney 1992

Appendices

Bibliography

1   Abram, Wm. Alex, History of Blackburn, 1870
2   The County Archives, Preston, Lancashire
3   Atkins, Richard Journal, 1792 – 1819
4   Australian Dictionary of Biography
5   Australian Encyclopaedia
6   Australian Scrap Book 1777 - 1866 NLA
7   Banks, Sir Joseph, Papers, Vol. 22
8   Barnard, Marjorie, Macquarie's World, 1946
9   Barrington, George, Voyage to NSW 1801
10   Barton, G. B. & Britten, Alex, History of NSW from the records 1894
11   Barton, G. B., The true Story of Margaret Catchpole, 1924
12   Barton, G. B., Newspaper story, Evening News, Sydney, 1898
13   Bentham, Jeremy, Principles of Penal Law, 1789
14   Bigge, John T., Oral and Written Evidence Report, ed. John Ritchie, 1971
15   The Bishop's Transcripts, Blackburn parish registers
16   Blackburn Parish Church Records
17   Blainey, Geoffrey, The Tyranny of Distance, 1966
18   Bondwick, James, First Twenty Years of Australia, London, 1882
19   Bowd, D., Macquarie Country, 1978
20   Census of NSW, Nov. 1828, Sainty M. R. & Johnson, K., 1980
21   Chapman Papers, Macquarie Letters, 1819
22   Clark, C. Manning, Select Documents in Australian History
23   Clark, C. Manning, A Discovery of Australia, 1976
24   Clark, C. Manning, Sources of Australian History OUP, 1957
25   Clark, C. Manning, A History of Australia, 1981
26   Clune, Frank, Bound for Botany Bay, 1964
27   Cobbold, Richard, The History of Margaret Catchpole, 1846
28   Cobley, John, Sydney Cove 1791 – 1792, A&R
29   Cobley, John, The Convicts, 1788 – 1792, Wentworth Press, 1965
30   Collins, David, An Account of the English Colony
31   Colonial Musters and Census Records
32   Cunninghum, Peter, Two Years in NSW, 1827
33   East India Co. Records Orbit House London, 1980
34   Emancipists' Petition, 1821
35   English Social History, ed. 1960

36 Examiner, Tasmanian Daily Newspaper, Launceston, 1870
37 Fletcher, Brian, Landed Enterprises and Penal Society
38 Fletcher, Brian, David Collins, RAHS 1976
39 Flinders and Price, Gov. Hunter's Papers
40 Forde, J. M., Genesis of Common Sense in Australia
41 Grose, Francis, Gov. Recorded Letters HRNSW
42 Halliday, Bibliography on Blackburn
43 Historical Records of Australia
44 Historical Records of NSW
45 Leroy, Paul Edwin, Emancipists from Prison to Freedom, Ann Arbor
46 MacArthur, Elizabeth, Letters
47 Nepean District Historical Society, Reibeycroft
48 Newgate Calendar 1782 – 1853
49 Palemr, F. A., Freeman's Reach and the Cattai
50 Plumb, J. H., England in the 18th Century, Vol. 7
51 Raven, Captain Wm., Letters HRNSW
52 Salmon, M., Pioneer Australians, newspaper cuttings
53 Shaw, J. G. Bits of old Blackburn, 1889
54 Sydney Morning Herald, 1831
55 Trevelyan, G. M., Illustrated English Social History, Vol. 3 & 4
56 Tasmanian Historical Research Journals
57 Thompson, George, Gunner, An Account of the miseries, 1794
58 Ward, Russell, The Australian Legend, 1958
59 Watson, Frederick,The Begining of the Government of Aust.

Index

Nance Irvine OAM

For Nance Capper Irvine an abiding interest in the first residents of the Sydney Rocks area was aroused in the late twenties during her daily climb, for five years, up through the Rocks to Fort Street Girls' High School, now the National Trust headquarters. Her story had to wait during the long years of family matters, teaching and clarinet playing in Newcastle. Between 1963 and 1974 she completed three further degrees including a M.Ed. (Sydney) and an Associate's year of study at London University. Retiring in 1977 from lecturing at Canberra C.A.E., she has found time for her four loves, music, literature, travelling and gardening, for lecturing part time for the Australian National University's Centre for Continuing Education in Comparative Literature and Music and for researching the historical background of Mary Reibey.

Last year she was honoured by the University of Canberra with a Master of Arts Causa Honoris for outstanding service to scholarship allied to her service to society as well as her contributions to Australian literature. She regards this as her greatest honour.

In 1988 Nance received the Order of Australia Medal for services to Literature and was invited to meet H.M. the Queen and H.R.H. Duke of Edinburgh.

Her books include two editions of *Mary Reibey, Molly Incognita, The Depression and Nellie Melba,* and *The Serius Letters.* Mrs. Irvine is the author of the children's play *Sydney Cove Adventures* currently being aired on BBC 4.